TWENTIETH CENTURY MISSIOLOGY

Timothy Yates with Stephen Skuce

cliff
COLLEGE
PUBLISHING

ISBN 978-1-898362-42-5
© 2014 Cliff College Publishing

British Library Cataloguing in Publication Data.
A catalogue record for this book is available
from the British Library.

**Cliff College Publishing,
Calver, Hope Valley, Derbys S32 3XG**

Printed by:

tel: 0115 932 0643 web: www.moorleys.co.uk

from data supplied electronically

DEDICATION

In recognition of the members of the International Association for Mission Studies in appreciation for much intellectual stimulus and warm friendship.

ACKNOWLEDGEMENTS

The dedication of this book to the International Association for Mission Studies and its membership represents my indebtedness to this body for its stimulus and friendship over nearly thirty years since my first attendance at the Harare meeting of 1985. There I presented my first paper to a group which included David Bosch, G. H. Anderson, C.F. Hallencreutz and other members: it appears as chapter 4 in the present collection. I must also express appreciation to those members of the mission academic community who have arranged for some of this material to be presented in their settings in lecture form: Professor Wilbert Shenk (Fuller Theological Seminary) Professor Kajsa Ahlstrand (University of Uppsala), and Dr Darrell Whiteman (Asbury Theological Seminary, Kentucky). My wife and I have received much kindness and hospitality on these visits. I must also express my thanks to the current editors of the journals where much of this material has appeared for their agreement to this publication: *Missiology*, *Mission Studies*, *Swedish Missionary Themes* (Svensk Missions Tidskrift), *Perspectives Missionnaires*, *Anvil* and, especially, the *International Bulletin of Missionary Research*. References to the occurrences in the journals will be found in the concluding footnotes of the papers. Finally, I must express my appreciation to Cliff College for their welcome as Methodists to a missiologist of a different tradition (Anglican) as lecturer and research supervisor over the last twenty years and their willingness to support this collection; to Lynne Firth for her secretarial help; and to Dr Stephen Skuce for his paper on D.T. Niles and much help with this text.

INTRODUCTION

Cliff College has become in recent years a major provider of mission studies and missiology courses. I was first invited to teach by the then principal, Dr Howard Mellor, who was able to link the college's work with the University of Sheffield in the 1990's: validation for degrees began in 1994. The college was inspected by the university for re-validation in 1999-2000, when the principal invited me with Dr Kenneth Cracknell and Dr Martyn Percy, to submit papers on the teaching of Christian mission for the assessors. These gave an enthusiastic endorsement of the college's work. Dr Mellor's successor in Dr Martyn Atkins, who had done much in his previous role as Director of Studies to strengthen and develop the teaching of mission with his colleague Dr Philip Meadows, made the decision to transfer validation to the University of Manchester and its Department of Christian Theology in 2004. Since then this university has facilitated Doctorates of Missiology from 2010, which can be taken by those engaged in forms of Christian ministry with a mixture of residential weeks and external study under approved supervisors. Further degrees on a full time basis have also resulted and the writer has been privileged to supervise both a Ghanaian Anglican to doctoral qualification and a Zimbabwean Methodist to a further degree since 2010.

In an earlier publication *Christian Mission in the Twentieth Century* I noticed the absence of schools of missiology in this country by comparison with South Africa, North America, Germany, Holland and Scandinavia, despite LesslieNewbigin's judgement on the subject: 'missiology, a discipline without which no training for the Christian ministry can be considered adequate for today's world'. Recently the University of Birmingham have had a notable Professor of Mission in Professor Werner Ustorf, now succeeded by Professor Allan Anderson, and the University of Edinburgh has a Professor of World Christianity in Dr Brian

Stanley, following the pioneering work of there of Professor Andrew Walls, who has also been a mentor and external examiner at Cliff College. Under its present principal, Dr Blake, and (until 2014) its Academic Dean, Dr Stephen Skuce, the college has made a significant contribution to the missiological scene in the UK. It is very gratifying that the college has proved willing to share in the publication of these papers and to contribute to them on the notable Asian Methodist missiologist, D.T. Niles.

Timothy Yates

CONTENTS

Issues and Thinkers

PART I ISSUES

PART II THINKERS

PART I

ISSUES

CHAPTER 1

EDINBURGH REVISITED: the tradition of Edinburgh 1910 and the approach to other faiths

The centenary of the great Edinburgh conference has now been and gone. Edinburgh 2010 has provided us with some important publications, not least Brian Stanley's volume *The World Missionary Conference, Edinburgh 1910* and a notable atlas from Todd Johnson and Kenneth Ross in *Atlas of World Christianity*, which follows the earlier *Statistical Atlas of Christian Missions* of the 1910 conference.[1]

What follows is an attempt to capture the spirit and tradition of Edinburgh, first by reference to nine published volumes of reports of the commissions, still a fascinating quarry for any concerned with the situation of the church in our own day, with many sidelights on such issues as theological training (V, 240-5), women in ministry (V, 148-51), revival (I), recreation for Christian workers (III, 323) and how to combine faith with realism when facing a budget deficit as a missionary society (VI, 211). Secondly, I will attempt to get behind the published reports to the spirit of Edinburgh as expressed by missionaries in the field, whose returns to questionnaires, still unpublished, provided the essential background to a conference which, without them, could not have reflected so deeply on the universal task of the church.

Edinburgh 1910: mission as strategy

Today we would be likely to be embarrassed by the range and extent of a triumphalist strain in the Edinburgh report, although when we look at the returns from missionaries for Commission IV on 'The Missionary Message', we shall find a rather different spirit prevails. The emphasis on world-wide strategy, to be pursued in quasi-military terms, can be illustrated by the frequent use of the term 'aggressive' in the reports. On one occasion only is this

---

[1] Brian Stanley, *The World Missionary Conference, Edinburgh 1910* (Grand Rapids: Eerdmans, 2009); Todd Johnson and Kenneth R. Ross, *Atlas of Global Christianity* (Edinburgh: Edinburgh University Press, 2009).

3

western emphasis redressed: 'the West has so exalted and given supreme emphasis to the aggressive and positive types of character that these have become highly enthroned among our cardinal virtues, so that we look with suspicion and contempt upon the ideal of the other hemisphere which does not reveal these. We speak of the mild Hindu and regard him as hardly worthy of our respect. We forget that the passive virtues, which have shone with such exclusive lustre in India, are as truly a part of our life as taught and exemplified by Christ, as are the assertive, aggressive virtues which have been so emphasised by us'.[2] With this notable exception, the reports and speeches use the term 'aggressive' everywhere in a commendatory sense, to express the world-wide advance which was needed. This is especially the case in Commission I, 'Carrying the Gospel to the non-Christian world', chaired by John Mott himself, but not exclusively so. The survey of the fields was judged to give a 'reliable basis for a comprehensive and aggressive policy' with the 'best disposition of the forces outlined'.[3] The church should 'resolutely attack' the 'great citadels of the non-Christian world' and its 'hitherto impregnable fortresses'[4] in its prosecution of its task in unoccupied or neglected fields. The church needed to build up its own spiritual life in to 'be an aggressive force'.[5] Field after field was said to be in need of 'aggressive work'. Islam, a major preoccupation at Edinburgh 1910, required 'the peaceful message of the Christian gospel' but through 'aggressive strategy (which) has ever been the most successful'.[6] The 'battle' was on for the Far East in this connection (G. Warneck)[7] and aggressive advance was needed in Thailand (then Siam) and Laos.[8] In the Near East, reinforcements were needed 'to mount an aggressive and not merely a defensive missionary campaign',[9] not merely guerrilla warfare' but a unified

---

[2]World Missionary Conference 1910, *Reports I-X* (Edinburgh: Oliphant, Anderson and Ferrier, 1910) III, p. 260 (hereafter E, I etc.).
[3]E, I, p. 2.
[4]E, I, p. 296.
[5]E, I, p. 369.
[6]E, I, p. 21.
[7]E, I, p. 435.
[8]E, I, p. 365.
[9]E, I, p.186.

spiritual campaign.[10] In India among *pariahs*, the Bishop of Madras made the same kind of comment in a Hindu context: with sufficient missionary forces to mount a 'prompt, aggressive and adequate campaign' thirty million people could be brought into the Christian church over the next fifty years.[11]One SPG missionary and college principal remarked that, if a policy of 'Christian atmosphere' was to be contrasted to one of 'aggressive Christian evangelism', he knew which he preferred: 'I do not myself believe in the policy of Christian atmosphere', 'What we must have, if anything at all, is aggressive evangelistic work'[12] Missionary bodies were urged to 'organise the church of Christ into the aggressive army of the Lord'.[13]

Two things at least need to be said to criticism of this approach. The New Testament itself has such metaphors of battle and struggle: did not our Lord teach of the strong man armed, who must be bound if he is to be dispossessed (Lk. 11:21-2)? St Paul saw himself engaged in a war, a fight in which he did not engage as a shadow boxer (1Cor. 9:6) but brought into captivity everything which was an obstacle to the knowledge of God, with weapons of war able to 'destroy strongholds' (1 Cor. 10:4 RSV). Both Ephesians and the Pastorals call on the Christian to fight the good fight of faith (Eph. 6:1; I Tim. 6:12) and church history has demonstrated the hold of the language of struggle on the Christian mind, with the baptized as soldiers in Christ's army ('manfully to fight under his banner', BCP) and, more recently, with a Salvation Army and a Church Army in which to enrol.

Aggression, however, is not a word with which we are at ease today. Unlike those delegates of 1910, we are post-Freudians and inheritors of two world wars. We prefer thoughts of peaceful penetration, and seek to express evangelism in these terms: 'the stress falls less on outward activity and more on inward quality, a sensitive responsiveness to the Sender, a readiness to move or to

---

[10]E, I, p. 190.
[11]E, I, p. 148.
[12] E, III, p. 417.
[13]E, VI, p. 169.

wait, to speak or to be still. The call to mission becomes ever less of a warrant for aggressive activity, let alone pentagon-like strategy of world domination'.[14] Nevertheless, understanding evangelism and the coming of the kingdom as warfare may remain an inescapable metaphor so long as sin, evil and the worldly powers are resistant to the claims of Christ. Neither must we allow the use of a particular kind of metaphorical language to blind us to the evidence it gives of commitment to making Christ known, which was at the heart of Edinburgh 1910.[15]

Secondly, when one turns to the response sent in by missionaries working in the field, there is a less hostile or pugnacious attitude revealed, for example, to other religions. The policy of 'attack' is explicitly disowned. It may even be that, at least in the case of Commission I, the language of world-wide assault owed more to the home-based strategists – whom one writer has called the 'ordained generals', though here they were often laymen[16] - over against the more moderating views of the missionaries in the field, who were aware that any wholesale 'attack' on other religious traditions was a very poor way of advancing Christ's claims among their adherents.

Pluralism: Edinburgh 1910 as a guide to a world of many faiths

As we turn from this world-conquering mood, an inescapable part of Edinburgh 1910, what guidance, if any, can the conference papers give in present religious pluralism? Here certain source documents exist which are of considerable value in any approach to those of alternative religious traditions. E. J. Sharpe, who wrote on one of the Edinburgh respondents from the field, J. N. Farquhar,

---

[14] S. Barrington-Ward, *CMS Newsletter*, no. 412, September 1977.
[15] John Mott was chairman of Commission I. His love of military metaphors has been noticed by commentators. For example, at a Student Volunteer Movement meeting of 1898 his closing speech was 'full of metaphors of the battlefield' Clifton Phillips in J. K. Fairbank (ed.) *The Missionary Enterprise in China and America* (Cambridge, Mass.: Harvard University Press, 1974), p. 102; cf. similar examples and comments on them pp. 101, 111, 114, 354.
[16]*Ibid.*, p. 288: the writer is Shirley Garrett in the symposium.

drew attention in his work to manuscript material behind Edinburgh which remained 'virtually untouched'.[17] This was certainly unfortunate, as it is a rich source. D. S. Cairns, who had been put in charge of Commission IV on the missionary message well enough in advance of the conference in 1908 to be able to circulate questionnaires to many workers in the fields, laid up his copies of the returns at Christ's College Library in Aberdeen,[18] used by him for writing the report for Commission IV 'The Missionary Message in relation to Non-Christian Religions', generally regarded then and since of 'exceptional quality'.[19] If, speaking very broadly, Jerusalem 1928 erred too greatly in the direction of an unqualified 'Yes' to the other religious traditions as the voice of IMC, paving the way for the syncretism of the 1930s, while Tambaram 1938 and Hendrik Kraemer's great preparatory volume appeared to many to say a resounding 'No', then Edinburgh 1910 as represented by the respondents to Cairns contained an admirable blend of Yes and No, written by men of great experience in the field and long acquaintance with, for example, Islam and Hinduism. They were asked various questions, notable among them being what attitude they judged the preacher should adopt, what supposed points of contact existed with the religions concerned, what constituted the greatest points of appeal in the Christian gospel. [20] We shall concentrate of the responses from those working in either an Islamic or Hindu context.

---

[17] E. J. Sharpe, *Not to Destroy but to Fulfil* (Lund: Gleerup, 1965) p. 276.
[18] Copies of the returns to D. S. Cairns can also be found in the Missionary Research Library, New York and the Yale Divinity School.
[19] B. Stanley, *The World Missionary Conference, Edinburgh 1910*, p. 245; Ch. 8 of this work gave extended and welcome treatment of Cairns and the commission.
[20] E, IV, p. 2.

The appeal of Jesus Christ

First, there is a continued reiteration in the responses of the appeal of Jesus himself to the unbeliever. It is the portrait of Jesus in the gospels which attracts, linked in the Indian returns very strongly with the teaching of the Sermon on the Mount and the living out of this teaching in the events of the passion, as in the prayer 'Father, forgive them'. So, C. F. Andrews, perhaps the most widely known missionary in India, wrote that the 'pure ideal picture of Jesus Christ in the Gospels is to the educated Hindu... the greatest of all attractions to the faith'.[21] A. G. Hogg, very different from Andrews in his expression of Christian faith at many points, is at one with him in this assessment: 'by far the strongest power of appeal is that which resides in the personality and life of Jesus'.[22] Whereas a 'body of divinity' does not attract a Hindu mind 'Christ himself is becoming an increasing attraction and a growing power' wrote T. E. Slater.[23] This assessment is given added weight by the testimony of various Hindu converts: Canon Nihal Singh wrote that 'the unsullied life of our Lord and his self-denial and the conquest of _self_ upon the cross are the elements which appeal most... Matthew 5 and the teaching of our Lord made a special appeal to me when I was a Hindu'.[24] R. C. Sircar also spoke of the drawing power of the Sermon on the Mount which led to his receiving Christ: he added the interesting additional feature that he was drawn _both_ by the tolerance of his Hinduism _and_ by the exclusiveness of Christianity, but it was the reading of the Sermon on the Mount that led to his receiving Christ.[25] The love, patience, gentleness and meekness of Christ have the greatest appeal, with the Sermon on the Mount and especially the Beatitudes (W. E. S. Holland).[26] Altogether it is Christ, not Christianity, which appeals to the Indian.[27]

---

[21] Aberdeen Returns for Commission IV (hereafter A, India etc). There are three volumes of responses from missionaries in India, cited in A, India I; and one from those in Islamic contexts.
[22] A, India I, no. 176, p. 53.
[23] A, India III, no. 229, p. 5.
[24] A, India III, no.211, p. 10.
[25] A, India III, no. 234, p. 42; cf. S. K. Rudra similarly no. 261, p. 4.
[26] A. India II, no. 177, p. 4.
[27] A, India III, no. 251, p. 7.

The same note is present in the returns from Islam, though it is less prominent. S. G. Wilson, then principal of a theological college in Persia and with thirty years' experience in the field, wrote: 'the greatest power of appeal (is)... the character of Jesus Christ his gentleness, his humility, purity, love and self-sacrifice, and with this the precepts of brotherly love'.[28]

The Doctrine of the Trinity

It is interesting that, long before the writing of Karl Barth or Lesslie Newbigin had reasserted the central importance of the doctrine of the Trinity for Christian proclamation; before, too, the debates as to whether the World Council of Churches itself should be Trinitarian rather than Christological in its confession: the responses show missionaries of the stature of Temple Gairdner and S. M. Zwemer making eloquent pleas for the reinstatement of an understanding of the Trinity which would make it religiously central. The same emphasis is present from workers in the Islamic and in the Hindu fields, although the former felt it more acutely. For W. H. Campbell, working in South India, the Trinitarian emphasis was 'essential' to counteract Indian monism and its failure. To him, the Trinity is 'a necessity for faith' against such a background.[29] Similarly, Edwin Greaves, working in the Hindu 'capital' of Benares (Varanasi) in North India, had come to regard the Trinity as 'vital', 'philosophically absolutely necessary' and for life 'full of warmth and power'.[30] It was this warmth and religious vitality that Temple Gairdner wanted to recapture in the context of Islam and his reflections found their way into Cairns' digest for the Commission. For Gairdner, the Trinity 'sums up' the Christian gospel but it needs to be preached with spiritual and ethical, rather than simply metaphysical, form. Islam 'forces the Christian church to find the Trinity in our heart; and it forces us to find the Trinity in the heart of God...the Christian who preaches the Trinity must

---

[28] A, Islam, no. 342, p. 275; cf. J. C. Young of the Keith Falconer Mission at Aden: 'the sinlessness of Jesus I would assuredly put first, then his tender, loving sympathy for sinners' no. 282, p. 296, i.e. 'first' in appeal to Muslims.
[29] A, India I, no. 33, p. 17.
[30] A, India I, no. 166, p. 13.

9

know the secret of the trinitarian life'. The emphasis on a Trinitarian Christianity, which expresses itself in prayer, devotion and worship, can be found suggestively delineated in Leonard Hodgson's fine book *The Doctrine of the Trinity*, which sets out what Gairdner is suggesting here.[31] Like Gairdner, the equally respected missionary to Islam, S. M. Zwemer, found in the Trinity and the atonement 'the heart of Christianity', a matter of which he was 'more than ever assured'.[32]

The approach to other religions

Here, inevitably, there is some variety of emphasis, both over the returns as a whole and within the body of material given to either tradition. First, from Islam, various missionaries stress that care should be taken not to attack Islam.[33] Somewhat in contrast to the Hindu returns, however, the emphasis of the most experienced missionaries is negative towards Islam, despite their pleas for sympathy and understanding. One missionary admits to a greater sense of theocentricity in his practice of Christianity through his exposure to the stress on theocentricity in Islam[34] but more typical is Temple Gairdner's complaint of the rarity of a spiritual, as distinct from a formal, outlook among Muslims. He has found it, 'but how rare!'[35] He cannot accept talk of Islam as a *preparatio evangelica*. Instead, it is self-confessedly a religion which regards itself as superseding Christianity towards its destruction. Gairdner, who was an essentially sensitive and profound student of Islam, respected as such by Muslims in Egypt, was joined in this negative assessment by two well-known missionaries in Northern Nigeria, T. E. Alvarez and Dr. W. R. Miller. They complain of lack of conscience in Muslims. Any points of contact are very superficial. W. A. Shedd, an able American missionary who worked in Persia, also saw the danger of superficial resemblances, but perhaps

---

[31] E, IV, pp. 153f.; cf. p. 135. L. Hodgson, *TheDoctrine of the Trinity* (London: Nisbet, 1943) pp. 176-94.

[32] A, Islam, no.283, p. 314.

[33] A, Islam, no. 258, p. 5 (Herman Barnum); cf. no. 259, p. 10 (James Cantine).

[34] A, Islam, no. 237, pp. 21f. (vanEss).

[35] A, Islam, no. 263, p. 24; no. 300, pp. 101, 107.

10

expresses more than any the characteristic attitude of both 'Yes' and 'No' which came from Edinburgh. 'So far as old faiths are true they should of course be confirmed; so far as they are defective' it is necessary to 'remove the erroneous...to secure a hearing for the gospel. This involves more stress on differences than on agreements'.[36]

The Indian returns, mainly from workers in Hindu surroundings, show a wide variety of views. Certainly, there were here more respondents who belonged to the 'fulfilment' school, of whom J. N. Farquhar was the most notable. Equally, there were some critics of this approach, outstanding among them, both for the rigour of his mind and the interest of his own theological odyssey, the Scottish missionary and theologian A. G. Hogg. For purpose of clarity we may divide these responses in three categories: (1) those where the Yes prevails (2) those where the Yes and No are held in balance; and (3) those where the No prevails over the Yes.

(1)   Francis Kingsbury, a convert from Hinduism from Madurai, wrote with echoes of Paul's speech at Lystra (Acts 14:15-18) that the missionary should be 'glad to find that God has not left Himself without witness in India'. We should be prepared to admit that 'there have been many sages and saints among the Hindus, men who have known God and have lived with Him'. For Kingsbury, Jesus is 'not destroyer but fulfiller', although he conceded that there are 'teachings and practices which should be severely and fearlessly condemned'.[37] This strongly positive reaction is present in others. N. C. Mukerjee notes the contrast between the two religions but holds that they have a secondary, if legitimate, place to points of agreement.

(2)   Perhaps we should not be surprised to find two Anglican bishops as proponents of the *via media* theologically. Both the Anglican bishop of Madras (Henry Whitehead) and the bishop of Calcutta (R. S. Copleston) put an equal emphasis

---

[36]A, Islam, no. 272, pp. 157f.
[37] A, India, II, no. 187, p. 4.

11

on the Yes and the No towards Hindu tradition.[38] The missionary must seek out points of contact while yet putting emphasis on points of divergence (Madras). The other religions are '*helps* so far as they tend to reveal or heal the corruption; *hindrances* so far as they are a screen, more or less consciously held up, between the human conscience and the demands of the Truth'. 'What is good in the non-Christian religion is often set up as a "screen": the better it is, the more fit it is to be alleged as a reason why a hearing should not be given to the *more imperative but similar* demand which Christianity makes.[39] Other non-episcopal figures take a similarly balance view. 'Many of the great truths of Christianity have their complement in Hinduism. But the truths of Hinduism are exaggerated and distorted out of all recognition'. The need is to 'set Hindu fragments in the "new light" of Christianity' and to bring 'half-neglected truths into prominence or aspects of truths into new perspective' (L. B. Chamberlain).[40] Again, 'we ought to strive to show how Christianity fulfils the highest aspirations of their hearts and completes the truths which are found in Hinduism, but Hinduism is a corruption of God's truth…distorted and discoloured through corroding and disintegrating influences'.[41]

(3) A sharper note of dissent and emphasis on the No came from A. G. Hogg. Hogg had an interesting theological and spiritual pilgrimage. This found its way, but without his name attached, into Cairns' digest for Commission IV. It is

---

[38] Whitehead was the brother of A. N. Whitehead, the philosopher and mathematician and was bishop of Madras 1899-1922. Copleston had been translated from Colombo in 1902 and was bishop of Calcutta 1902-1913: M. E. Gibbs, *The Anglican Church in India 1600-1700* (New Delhi: ISPCK, 1972) pp. 309n, 411f.
[39] A, India I, no. 235, pp. 5-6; II, no. 209, p. 11 (my italics).
[40] A, India I, no. 134, pp. 11-12.
[41] A, India I, no. 130, pp. 14-15.

Hogg who is described as a 'teacher in a large college',[42] who had arrived in India with a vague theism, prepared to surrender 'alleged facts of the New Testament narratives – even the resurrection itself' provided that the general impression 'of Jesus' personality was not affected'. He wrote: 'I had not long been in India when a radical change began to be effected in the tendency of my thinking'. Surrounded by Hindu students and literature, he became convinced that two things were fundamental to Christianity: God as active will, self-expressed in history and supremely in Jesus Christ; and the need to 'break root and branch' with 'the conception of human merit' over against Hindu doctrine of *karma*, which was essentially worked out in terms of desert. With this theological pilgrimage as his background, Hogg sharply repudiated 'fulfilment' themes: 'Christian doctrines are not the fulfilment of Hindu doctrines': 'outside the region of vague abstraction, what does it (fulfilment) mean?' Hindu satisfaction 'certainly proves that Christian beliefs fulfil the yearning of the Hindu consciousness thrown out of equilibrium by Christian influence, but not that Christianity is a fulfilment to...the typical undisturbed Hindu consciousness'. Christianity 'is the solution of a religious problem which the typical Hindu does not feel but which, under favourable conditions, he can be made to feel'. 'If this be the real relation of Christianity to Hinduism, to call it one of fulfilment may be...permissible but the description obscures the fact that it fulfils by, at least partially, destroying'.[43] Others, apart from Hogg, were critical of fulfilment ideas but he is the most rigorous critic. A missionary called Gulliford wrote: 'we must not be content with trying to show that Christ fulfils Hinduism and Islam as he fulfilled Judaism',[44] a task which

---

42 E, IV, p.207. A, India II, no. 176, p. 59-60 describes his change of view in full. Cf. J. L. Cox, 'The Missionary Thought of A. G. Hogg' Ph.D.thesis University of Aberdeen, 1977, note 7 et al.
43 A, India II, no. 176, p. 14.
44 A, India II, no. 168, p. 7.

Pannikkar and others have assayed to do in such works as *The Unknown Christ of Hinduism* (London: Darton, Longman and Todd, 1964). Another missionary, J. P. Jones, while noting that both religions have a stress on divine incarnation which is unique to themselves, continued: 'this consonance passes into dissonance'.[45] It becomes plain that Hendrik Kraemer's massive critique of fulfilment ideas in his *Christian Message in a Non-Christian World* (London: Edinburgh House Press, 1938) had a history of missionary disquiet behind it from a much earlier generation of thinkers.

Conclusion

What conclusions can be drawn from this, inevitably highly compressed, account of the Edinburgh 1910 tradition? First, whether or not the missionary task is expressed in the language of struggle and in metaphors of the battlefield, the reality to which these figures of speech witnessed of deep commitment to the world-wide proclamation of the gospel is as relevant as ever. Secondly, in so far as the missionaries' returns from the field comprised the foundational material for Edinburgh's findings, certain emphases from Commission IV remain fundamental: the unique attraction of the Jesus Christ of the Gospels to those of other traditions remains paramount and suggests, among other things, that the great efforts of translators to convey that portrait in the languages of the recipients is essential and well directed. The attraction which Jesus had for Hindus and Muslims at the turn of the century has been amply exemplified in our own day by those and other seekers after truth. Secondly, the returns have shown the need for Christian doctrinal formulations, as in the doctrine of the Trinity, as a *missionary* obligation, where doctrine and religious expression cannot be lost sight of. A sharper focus and expression will result when Christian doctrine, held in the person of the missionary, is in immediate relation to non-Christian systems and persons, providing a fresh stimulus to work out the importance for Christian life and practice, as was the case for Temple Gairdner

---

[45] A, India II, no. 184, p. 14. An earlier version of this article appeared in *The Churchman*, vol. 94, no. 2, 1980, pp. 145-155.

and S. M. Zwemer. Finally, in confronting the pluralism of the modern world, the material reveals the need to contain and reflect upon the sheer variety of Christian responses to other religions and ideologies. This variety was present at Edinburgh and has become more sophisticated and diverse since. Edinburgh's emphasis, the combination of the Yes and the No, of genuine sympathy and yet also rigorous criticism, applied to the Christian tradition as well as to that of others, is greatly needed. So is the diversity of reaction between traditions and the attempt to distinguish seriously in each separate case which of the Yes and the No should preponderate and why. For such an approach, Edinburgh provided much material of lasting value

CHAPTER 2
CHRISTIAN APPROACHES TO OTHER RELIGIOUS TRADITIONS
The International Review of Missions 1912-1939

The preparatory papers for the 1910 Edinburgh Conference, as represented especially by the returns made by missionaries in the field to D.S. Cairns for Commission IV on the Missionary Message, had shown the wide differences of view among thoughtful Christians in their estimate of other religious traditions. The returns varied between the 'yes' of broad acceptance of the authenticity of the experience of God in other households of faith to outright rejection, from the emphasis on fulfilment to a repudiation of it as a proper category to be employed.[46] The report reflected upon some of this diversity of view in the section produced under Cairns' chairmanship. Apart from setting up the Continuation Committees in various parts of the world, one of the most significant results of Edinburgh 1910 was the birth of the *International Review of Missions*, which began appearing in 1912, as a journal in which practising missionaries, academics and thinking Christians of all races, not least among the so-called 'younger churches', could share their missionary ideas and concerns. Prominent among these was the question of the missionary message and the approach to the other religions.

J.H. Oldham, who had been so influential in the success of the Edinburgh Conference, now showed his immense value to the missionary movement by his visionary yet capable editorship of the IRM. In the first issue of 1912 he was quick to point out that, 'among the subjects demanding serious study, one of the most important is the Missionary Message in relation to each of the non-Christian religions'.[47] It was not enough to do an exercise in

---

[46] Returns to D.S. Cairns for Commission IV of the Edinburgh conference, available at Christ's College, Aberdeen, and the Day Missions Library, Yale Divinity School.
[47] *IRM 1912*, p. 3. All the references below are to the composite volumes of the *International Review of Missions* made up of the issues for that year.

comparative religion. What was needed was to find 'in actual experience (what is) ... Really living ... as distinct from that which is merely traditional and formal' in the other tradition: and, with that, what are the 'vital forces of the gospel as it comes in contact with non-Christian peoples' and 'what aspects of it possess the greatest power of appeal'.[48] This was a period when the shadow of advancing Islam, especially in Africa, exercised the minds of missionary thinkers; and it was not surprising that the first great religious tradition addressed by Oldham as editor was Islam. Articles under the title of 'The Vital Forces of Islam' appeared in the early issues of 1912 and 1913 by such figures as Temple Gairdner, W.A. Shedd, Pastor Gottfried Simon, Professor Stewart Crawford, Suraj-ud-Din (a Moslem convert), Godfrey Dale and Professor Duncan Black McDonald, a leading academic authority on Islam of the day.[49] The writers, as might be expected, refer back to the early Christian apologists and Greek and Latin Fathers in their confrontation with religious pluralism in the first centuries of the Christian era. Duncan Black McDonald took the Logos doctrine of the Alexandrian fathers and felt after a link between the Moslem insistence on the Qu'ran as God's word and the Logos. He had to concede that the Moslem emphasis was on 'oratio' rather than 'ratio', as in the Fathers: but his contribution raised the question as to how far Christian apologetic to Islam can treat the Qu'ran as, in some sense, a hypostatised entity, related to but apart from God himself, in the Moslem tradition?[50] Professor Mackichan, a principal of Wilson College, Bombay, and Vice Chancellor of the University of Bombay, also looked to Clement of Alexandria and believed that the Logos view could be embraced by all Christians. As the Christian studied Indian philosophical and religious literature 'there are gleams of truth which the Christian church ought to be ready to accept as an evidence of the diffused energy of the divine Logos... thoughts which sustained the philosophies of India through ages of profound spiritual seeking after God'. Nevertheless, he added, this sympathy 'need not blind

---

[48] Idem

[49] *IRM 1912* pp. 44-61, 279-293, 452-473, 601-617; *IRM* 1913 pp. 97-117, 305-317, 657-673.

[50] *IRM 1913* pp. 666, 672.

us to essential distinctions... let us not conceal from India that its religious history... has failed to lead it to the true knowledge of God'.[51] The 'gleams of light' view was also present in an article by a leading French religious anthropologist of the day, Henri Junod, as he reflected on his experience among Bantu peoples of southern Africa, this time by reference to the apologist Justin Martyr: 'if it be true that paganism is not simply a mixture of gloom and vice, if, as Justin Martyr contends, in the obscurity there are discernible streaks of light which foretell the advent of full day, the Gospel ought to be presented, not merely in its antagonism to pagan error, but also as fulfiller of former aspirations'. For the missionary such an approach will give a new interest in religions and will mean that he is 'no longer the theorist, teaching the idea of a superior race but the elder brother, guiding his younger brethren towards the hill of holiness, where the Father bids his children gather'.[52]

As in the case of the returns of 1908, it is interesting to notice that national Christians, even converts, seemed more accepting and affirmative of alternative religious traditions than the European contributors. So, in an early article in 1912, the Japanese contributor Tashuku Harada, president of a respected Christian educational institution, Doshisha College in Japan, wrote: 'for my part it is inconceivable that anyone who has impartially studied the history of religion can fail to admit the universality of the activity of the spirit of God and the consequent embodiment of a degree of truth in all faiths'.[53] Suraj-ud-Din, who had experienced himself a long and intense personal struggle between an inherited Islam and Christianity, showed a notable generosity, not always present in Christian converts towards the faith that they have left: he gave 'personal testimony' to 'the fact of having met with men of deep spiritual experiences in Islam, as well as with the phenomenon of lives made extremely sensitive to sin'.[54] Among Europeans, the

---

[51] *IRM 1914* pp. 247-8, 253.
[52] *IRM 1914* pp. 105-6.
[53] *IRM 1912* p. 91.
[54] *IRM 1913* p. 110. Cf Nicol Macnicol: 'we see (Hindu seekers) seeking not God's gifts but God himself...But dare we say there are no finders? 'I have tasted sweetness at his feet' says Tukaram'. *IRM 1916* p. 219.

Bishop of Calcutta (G.A. Lefroy) was one who showed appreciation, if qualified. He had been sent the composite volume of articles on 'the Vital Forces of Islam' to review. Once again there is reference to the Fathers, this time to Tertullian: 'the outstanding impression left on my mind...is the most welcome one of the wide prevalence, even in the Mohammedan world which so often seems singularly lacking in this aspect, of the *anima naturaliter Christiana*'. He was particularly commendatory of the article by Professor Stewart Crawford because he was able to show that his contact with Islam had illuminated his understanding of the New Testament 'and this not only negatively but also positively.'[55] Our contemporary emphasis that to immerse oneself in another religious tradition is to discover more deeply the truths of our own is not new. Nor, despite much triumphalism in the Edinburgh Conference reports, was the disclaimer of an approach from superiority: writing on Ramon Lull, the great medieval missionary to Islam, H.U. Weitbrecht gave as the approach to Islam 'to give the Moslem the best we have in the best way we can, with no assumption of superiority or right to censure, but in the attitude of friendly service.'[56]

In relation to Hinduism, this was the period of J.N. Farquhar's *Crown of Hinduism* (1913). As Eric Sharpe has shown in his study *Not to Destroy but to Fulfil* (1965), Farquhar was a leading exponent of the view, shared by other thinkers, that Christianity was best viewed as the fulfilment of the highest Hindu traditions, even as it had fulfilled the Jewish expectations of the Old Testament. Farquhar wrote in the IRM: 'during the past century Christianity has been like a great search-light flung across Hinduism. Only in that light, have all its weaknesses and corruptions stood out before man's eyes. But under the same light Hindus have once more discovered what they had almost forgotten, viz. the best parts of Hinduism... does not all this make it easier to apply the concept of fulfilment?'[57] Farquhar's approach, however, caused an uneasiness in other experienced and thoughtful

---

[55] *IRM 1915* pp. 319-20.
[56] *IRM 1915* p. 419.
[57] *IRM 1914* p. 427.

Indian missionaries. Mackichan, already noted for his appreciation of Clement of Alexandria and therefore no enemy, presumably, to a comprehensive approach, was critical in particular of the title of Farquhar's book. In his view it did not fairly describe the critically informed stance which Farquhar adopted in the content. By reference to the (to him) distorted title, Mackichan is clear that 'we are misleading India if we present to it the Christian gospel as the consummation of its distinctive religious development. Such a message brings no help to India, it only tends to confirm India in a mistaken estimate of its own spiritual achievement and to neutralise the effect of the *preparatio evangelica* through which India has been called to pass in the experience of its own religious history'.[58] As he had done earlier in his return to D.S. Cairns for the Edinburgh Conference, A.G. Hogg showed himself a rigorous, penetrating and incisive critic of Farquhar's approach in his review of 1914: 'doubtless Christ fulfils what is good in Hinduism. But he leaves out so much of what was in Hinduism and he fulfils so much of what was never in Hinduism that Mr Farquhar's tracing out of this aspect of fulfilment sometimes seems far-fetched'... 'what Christ directly fulfils is not Hinduism but the need of which India has begun to be conscious, the need of which he has made her begin to feel conscious, the need, by making her feel the need of which, he has made her no longer quite Hindu'. For Hogg, the message '"you need Christ now" is really more telling than "Christ fulfils your old religion". The latter can hardly be freed from condescension'.[59] It is a comment not too dissimilar to criticisms of Pannikkar's more recent approach, and that of Karl Rahner, in treating those of other traditions as 'anonymous Christians', which also runs the risk of Christian condescension. A.K. Reischauer, facing the Buddhist tradition, found himself in a similar position to Hogg, who elsewhere had asked if Christ did not first have to come as destroyer before he fulfilled: he described the Buddhism he knew in which he saw much good as 'leaning towers' in need of

---

[58] *IRM 1914* p. 250.
[59] *IRM 1914* pp. 172-3.

fresh foundations if Christianity were to provide a 'fulfilment' in any real sense.[60]

In the first thirteen years of the IRM's life there is only one article directly on the Christian message. Julius Richter's inaugural lecture to the faculty of theology at the University of Berlin 1912, as he took up the chair of Missions, was entitled 'Method of Missionary Apologetic'. It was, however, after 1925 that the theological treatment of the subject intensified, under the combined influences of Karl Barth and the 'theology of crisis'; the Jerusalem Conference of 1928 characterised by an accepting approach like that of Rufus Jones who had spoken of the other religions as 'allies in our quest for perfection' against an enveloping secularism; and the publication in 1932 of the Laymen's Foreign Mission Inquiry report, associated with the name of the American Professor of Philosophy at Harvard, W.E. Hocking. It was a period which culminated with the publication of Hendrik Kraemer's work *The Christian Message in a non-Christian World* (1938).

Richter had showed himself to be frankly exclusivist in his approach. He saw the great need for 'scientific treatment' in dealing with the question of the missionary relation between Christianity and the non-Christian religions: but 'Christianity is an exclusive religion. Wherever Christian missionary enterprise comes into contact with the non-Christian religions it sets itself to oust them… in the conviction that this is necessary to the salvation of their adherents'. As the bacilli of unbelief spread, even to the remote hamlets of Europe, the missionary needed to be made spiritually immune 'through the theological clarification of his Christian consciousness of the superiority of his religion to all others'. This was all the more needed as the then prevailing 'history of religions' school 'threatens to level down the religious conception of humanity to an unrelieved relativism'.[61] The emphasis on 'superiority' was taken up by H. Frick, a Professor of

---

[60] *IRM 1915* p.581. Cf. A.G. Hogg's Return to Cairns: Aberdeen documents India II no. 176 p.14.
[61] *IRM 1913* pp. 521, 523, 525, 528.

Systematic Theology in Germany. In an article of 1926 Frick tried to distinguish carefully between the superiority inherent in the gospel and any civilisation or culture to which the gospel gave rise. The 'daily routine of Westerners', as also the 'actual religious life of the churches' was on the same level as the other world religions. In Frick's account, our Christianity is 'fragile and treacherous' but even so we 'may not surrender the conviction of superiority': indeed, he added in italics, 'Christian missions must be based upon a conviction of the superiority of their message if they are to remain sound and honest'.[62] While commending Frick in general, A.K. Reischauer demurred at his *a priori* appeal to 'superiority'. What was needed was the empirical data of superiority of life and practice: 'we should not hamper our free enquiry by unnecessary assumptions as to superiority growing out of inherited beliefs as to the exclusiveness and finality of Christianity: such claims must vindicate themselves by the content of the message revealed and the type of life which a religion really fosters. At least that is what the demand of modern man would make of religion and the demand which a Christian would make of the adherents of other religions'.[63]

For William Paton, the second editor of IRM after J.H. Oldham, the effect of the Jerusalem Conference of 1928 had been 'slightly to minimize the importance of the non-Christian faiths, as already doomed to fall at the attacks of the secular movement'.[64] The conference called out two weighty articles on the subject from British theologians, however, D.S. Cairns and O.C. Quick being theologians of stature who both taught what would now be called systematic theology. Cairns wrote regretting that the returns to him for the Edinburgh Conference had not been published in full, because they provided a most 'vivid panorama of the actual condition of the religions of the world'. He noted how both the Edinburgh and Jerusalem Conferences had included sections on the missionary message, as neither Liverpool (1860) nor London (1888) had done. He recalled R.E. Speer's closing and meditatory

[62] *IRM 1926* pp. 625-646.
[63] *IRM 1928* pp. 123, 122.
[64] *IRM 1928* p. 438.

remarks at Edinburgh that 'just as early Christianity in the end preserved the best of Greek and Latin civilisation, so the signs today were that the greatest values of the non-Christian faiths would only survive as they became baptised into Christ'. For Cairns, 'about everything in the power of the Christian mission in fact depends on the finality and absoluteness of the Christian salvation, Jesus Christ is something much more than the greatest of the prophets. He is 'God manifest in the flesh', and Cairns commended both William Temple and J.A. Mackay for making this clear in their papers at the Jerusalem meeting. Mackay was also right in calling for the missionary movement to be more theological, not primarily for the 'missioned' but for 'the Church itself and the missionaries who represent her'.[65]

O.C. Quick's is probably the outstanding article on our subject in the entire period of 1912-1939. It deserves to be read and studied in full still as a seminal and brilliant handling of some of the great issues of inter-faith relationships. Quick perceived that the two principles of uniqueness and universality threatened to conflict. For the old school of missionary thinker, all hung on uniqueness; for the newer school the emphasis was on fulfilment. Secularism was seen as the enemy. Its concomitant was a loss of objective authority in spiritual values, so that 'everywhere the principle of authority is being undermined by the subtle influence of this subjectivism': 'the only rule acknowledged is that of a relativity which is itself the negation of rule'. To Quick it was arguable that this was not the moment to criticise other religions: the advancing forces of scientific and secular education might be expected to provide solvents. But there is, nevertheless, a profound dissatisfaction with 'scientific relativism as a faith to live by' and a thoughtful rising generation admired Jesus, if not organised religion. This meant that, apart from any theological or theoretical reasons, there were 'strong practical reasons for refusing to compromise with the relativism which suggests that Christianity presents only one aspect of a many sided truth... This is not only false to the old gospel; it can only ignore, or even aggravate, the very need for the supply of which the world is already beginning to

---

[65] *IRM 1929* pp. 325, 330.

look again towards Christ'. So, the appearance of humility in 'abating the claims of Christianity' is 'really altogether deceptive…The Christian's humility can only truly be based on the ground that the Christian gospel is not his own but God's. In other words, it is precisely in so far as the Christian gospel is absolute, not relative to the preacher, that the preacher is able to proclaim it without in any way magnifying himself'.

> Quick reached for an analogy, which in my view brilliantly illustrated the replacement of the old exclusivism by a new inclusivism, without loss of the virtues of the old position but giving it a new and welcome inclusive expression. He invited his readers not to think in terms of solids displacing fluid: so often in the theology such 'matter-based' thinking was unhelpful. Instead we are to think of the action of light, which gives 'reflexion of itself at every point where the surface is capable of reflecting while at the same time it enriches its own purity by the variety of tints which it makes visible'. By this analogy, other religions should be seen in the light of the Christian gospel, revealed 'for the first time in their own best and truest colours; and, by being thus revealed, enhance and enrich the glory of the gospel itself'.
> Under such a proposal, to find a point of contact, even in a corrupt religion, was not to be relativist or syncretist. Rather, it is to find Christ (as ever unexpectedly) at Nazareth, despised by so being by the orthodox. For Quick such manifestations of true values as the scientists' sacrifices in the cause of truth or the Moslem's emphasis on international brotherhood or the Buddhist's sympathy for pain and suffering were tints of light, picked up by the light of the gospel and brought into a new and truer relief'.[66]

---

[66] *IRM 1928* pp.446, 448-452. O.C. Quick was Professor of Divinity first at the University of Durham and Regius Professor of Divinity at Oxford.

For the purposes of this review, Quick's article provides a theological climax, if not a conclusion. In the period 1930-39 at least two Barthian voices were raised in the IRM in Karl Hartenstein's article of the 'Theology of the Word and Missions' (1931) and J.A. Mackay's on the 'Theology of the Laymen's Foreign Missions Inquiry' (1933). The first pointed to the Cross, which 'reveals what man is, even 'good' man, namely a mutineer and a rebel against God, rejecting God's revelation'. This makes it dangerous to use the word 'fulfilment', that is, 'in any other sense than its original one, namely, that Christ is the fulfilment of Old Testament prophecy'. Missions needed also to avoid talking of a 'Christian' culture: 'we have learnt to think differently about superiority of our culture... it is today palpable how our culture is... under 'the law of death'.[67] Hartenstein's emphasis on the elements of struggle, the destruction of illusions and on decision were matched in Mackay by the stress on a Kierkegaardian 'either-or' replacing the 'both-and' of pre-Barthian theology. Rufus Jones and others had failed to recognise 'the sunset glow of nineteenth century romanticism'. Christianity needed not to buttress bourgeois society, with its paralysis of the will, but to provide instead a 'reactive' to 'produce a crisis'. Indeed, only a basically 'crusading' element was able to supply an alternative to the total demands of Fascism, communism and even the Group Movement (Buchmannism) and give a credible thrust to the Christian appeal.[68]

The stage was set for Hendrik Kraemers's *Christian Message in a non-Christian World*, published in 1938 as a preparatory volume for the Tambaram Conference of that year. While Mackay and Hartenstein struck the deep theological ground notes, K.S. Latourette, the great historian of Christian missions, drew attention to the tendency in the direction of syncretism as he reviewed the Laymen's Foreign Mission Inquiry in the same year of 1933. It was, he wrote, a product of 'left-centre' American Protestantism 'with its new aim for missions'. This was stated as 'to seek out with people of other lands a true knowledge and love of God, expressing in life and word what we have learned through Jesus

---

[67] *IRM 1931* pp. 223, 225.
[68] *IRM 1933* pp. 178, 180-181.

Christ and endeavouring to give effect to his spirit in the life of the world'. Latourette found here no Cross, no doctrine of the Atonement, no Resurrection or doctrine of the Holy Spirit; nor, ecclesiologically, any emphasis on ministry, creeds, sacraments or treatment of the church as the body of Christ.[69]

Finally, in 1939, the IRM included a moving appeal from C.F. Andrews for inclusiveness in a review article which was theologically critical of the a-historical and 'absorptive' view of Christ of a Hindu writer but at the same time drew attention to the inclusive attitudes of Jesus as expressed in Mark 3:33-35 and Matt. 25 where 'there is no note of exclusiveness. Every barrier is down' and Paul's insight about there being neither Jew nor Greek was upheld and commended as a true interpretation of his Master. Balancing this, the theologian H.H. Farmer gave evidence of how deeply Kraemer's ideas had influenced the Tambaram meeting in its view of other religions: 'considered as totalities... they are in a very real sense all wrong... despite, we repeat, ... actual and isolated rightnesses – for the reason that they leave, (and must leave without Christ), the basic problem of man's existence unsolved... the problem, namely, of his alienation from God through sin. Built upon another foundation, organised around another centre, they are radically and totally different; to say this is not in the first instance to make a judgement of value, it is merely to make a statement of plain fact'.[70] While D.S. Cairns gave open support and admiration to Kraemer's book in a review article, he wanted to raise certain criticisms in the context of his 'deep agreement with Dr Kraemer's main purpose' and his 'admiration for the quality of his book'. Cairns' review provides a suitable conclusion to this assessment of the IRM over these years on this subject, for he took up so many of the issues that have been noted above. If, he wrote, God is continuously with all peoples, as Kraemer claimed, 'are we to regard all religions as merely products of the human mind? Must there not be in them something from that which is above nature "bright shoots of everlastingness"'? Although Kraemer had not gone the whole way

---

[69] *IRM 1933* pp. 159, 160.
[70] *IRM 1939* p. 179; 1939 p. 259.

with Barth on other religions 'the Barthian element in his thought... seems to me not only in conflict with that more generous judgement of the non-Christian religions...but in plain conflict with many of the facts in the non-Christian religions themselves'. He examined Kraemer's view that all non-revelational religions are to be seen as monist naturism without any Logos-light in them: not only does the occurrence of 'tabu' in animist religions point beyond to an Absolute; but, in a major religious tradition like Zoroastrianism, there is a 'true, if imperfect, theism, so that Söderblom wrote of it 'not only is God one and moral but...history is not cyclical'. Cairns suggested that 'in Zoroast-er (God) found a servant who understood his Spirit better than did the Brahmans and so Persian religion rose and Indian religion lost its opportunity and fell to a lower plane'. He quoted J.W. Waterhouse, an authority on the subject, to the effect that, in Zoroastrianism, 'Ahura, the Creator, is one and his demands are ethical'. Cairns pointed also to 'bhakti' worship in India, Shin-shu in Japanese Buddhism (whose homilies he wrote 'bore an extraordinary resemblance to Christian preaching') and to the sages of Greece and Rome – Aeschylus, Socrates, Plato and Vergil in order to reiterate his view that 'in every nation he that fears God and works righteousness is accepted by him' (Acts 10:35).[71]

Having said all this, Cairns still concedes the great dangers of accommodation, never more so than in the present 'hour of danger', an allusion to the National Socialist State. Historically, it had taken the 'earthquake of the Reformation' to shake the church out of a situation where heathen practices, 'the jungle', had come back 'in roaring flood' into the 'hardly won clearings'. With this sobering reference to history Cairns ended on a note of strong commendation of Kraemer's work, which was on 'the great theme of Christian missions', displaying 'wide knowledge of the great world context', 'knowledge of the non-Christian faiths...and, above all, impelling faith'.[72]

---

[71] *IRM 1939* pp. 124-7, 129, 130-1.
[72] *IRM 1939* p. 132. This paper was published in *Mission Studies* Vol. VI/I, No. 11, 1989, pp. 41-50 and was a contribution to the Rome meeting of the IAMS of that year.

CHAPTER 3

CHRISTIAN CONVERSION 1902-1993
William James to Lewis Rambo

This paper has a limited intention. By re-visiting two classic treatments of the twentieth century and one more recent publication, it seeks to reassess the significance of conversion for mission studies. All three of the works have addressed the psychology of Christian conversion and, in doing so, have provided their readers with insight into the psychological impact of the Christian message on human personality and culture, whether within a broadly Christian cultural context or as a catalyst for change and transformation in primary fields of mission, those areas where in Paul's terms the missionary is preaching Christ 'where he has not been named.'[73]

Before examining these treatments further it may be as well to define what is, and what is not, to be considered. First, there is no attempt to deal with conversion as it appears in other religious traditions, though, for example, in our times Westerners are being drawn to Islam and Buddhism and will give an account of 'conversion' to these faiths which may well bear resemblances to what is described by our authorities. Secondly, conversion is not used as a term denoting change of denominational allegiance, as if to describe a Methodist who becomes a Roman Catholic. The subject is specifically conversion to Jesus Christ.

Such Christian conversion has its roots in the New Testament era, with the earliest accounts being given by Luke in Acts, those of Saul of Tarsus (given three times by Luke, presumably to emphasise it importance), Cornelius (given twice), the Ethiopian treasurer and eunuch, Lydia and the keeper of the gaol at Philippi.[74] In the cases of Saul and the gaoler these are explicitly

---

[73] Rom 15:20
[74] Ac 9:1-19,cf. 22:3-16, 26:9-18, 8:26-39, 10:34-48; cf. 11:4-17, 16:11-15, 16:25-34

conversions to the risen Christ and calls to action. So, Saul asks: 'Who are you Lord?' and the reply is: 'I am Jesus whom you are persecuting...go into the city and it will be shown you what you must do,' and the gaoler asks: 'What must I do to be saved?' and receives the answer: 'Believe in the Lord Jesus Christ and you will be saved with all your house.'[75] Cornelius is urged by Peter to trust in the crucified and risen Christ in order to receive forgiveness of sins.[76] While the idea of turning or returning to the Lord was common in the Old Testament (the Hebrew verb transliterated *shub* has 1,050 occurrences[77] and is taken up in the 39 uses of the verb *epistrephein* in the New Testament, as also in the use of *metanoein* in the preaching of John the Baptist and Jesus, describing in both cases a change of mind or direction and allied in Jesus' teaching to a call to recognise the advent of God's kingdom),[78] what differentiates Christian conversion is that the turning is towards the person of Christ. So, Lesslie Newbigin defined it as 'the inner turning of the heart and will to Christ'; but, in doing so, he is anxious to show that, as in the initial experience of Jesus' disciples in his earthly ministry, there remain three constituents to the experience: (1) a personal relation to him, (2) a visible community, (3) a pattern of behaviour. 'The inner turning of the heart and will,' he wrote, 'must neither be separated from, nor identified with, membership in the visible community and commitment to the pattern of behaviour.' The call to repentance and faith is a call to 'turn round in order to participate in this new reality,' that is, the kingdom of God, and is 'a commitment to action.'[79]

---

[75] Ac 9:5-6, 16:30-31
[76] Ac 10:39-43
[77] C. Brown (ed.), *New International Dictionary of New Testament Theology*, (Carlisle: Paternoster Press, 1997) p. 353.
[78] G. Kittel (ed.), tr. G. Bromiley, *Theological Wordbook* IV (Grand Rapids, MI: Eerdmanns, 1965) pp. 722-729.
[79] L. Newbigin, 'Conversion', in: *Concise Dictionary of the Christian World Mission* (London: Lutterworth Press, 1970) pp. 147-148.

I. William James

While the New Testament showed little interest in the psychology of conversion, with the emphasis, as Newbigin pointed out, on *action* rather than experience, the three twentieth century treatments here have all focused on this aspect. William James (1842-1910) was a philosopher who taught at Harvard. He was the elder brother of the novelist Henry James. They were sons of a father who had been strongly influenced by the Swedish theosophist Swedenborg. William James belonged to the school known as 'pragmatism', which had been defined as 'the doctrine that the test of the value of any assertion lies in its practical consequences.'[80] This gave him a natural interest in conversion, for conversion may be thought to provide empirical evidence that ideas have identifiable effects. In his work *Pragmatism* of 1907, James argued that 'true ideas are those that can be corroborated and verified...an idea is made true by events.'[81] The work by which William James is best remembered is his *Varieties of Religious Experience* of 1902, the Gifford lectures at Edinburgh, which one day were to cause Karl Barth some difficulty when invited to give them, for they are required to be given on 'natural religion'. The ninth and tenth lectures are specifically devoted to conversion, although the rest of the book has a good deal of material which relates to it. His treatment has been fairly criticised as highly individualistic: James' case studies are of individuals in North American or European contexts and relate to their personal experiences. There is little here of the second constituent noted by Lesslie Newbigin, as essential to Christian conversion, relationship to the visible community, although changes in behaviour get due recognition. James' distinction between the 'once born' and the 'twice born', which he borrowed from F.W. Newman, has attracted theological criticism: it is held, properly enough, that the New Testament looks for new birth for all, of which baptism is a sign.[82]

---

[80] M. Drabble (ed.), 'Pragmatism', in: *Concise Oxford Companion of English Literature* (Oxford: OUP, 1985) p. 452.
[81] R.T. Handy, 'Pragmatism', in: A. Richardson (ed.), *Dictionary of Christian Theology* (London: SCM Press, 1982).
[82] Jn 3:3-8; W. James, *Varieties of Religious Experience,* (Glasgow: Collins (1902), 1977) pp. 80-83.

'The distinction made by William James between once-born and twice-born Christians is a pretty epigram but poor theology. The New Testament knows only twice born Christians'.[83] Perhaps, however, there is some continuing validity in the phrase as it is used to distinguish between what are often called 'cradle Christians' and, for example, adult converts, who have sometimes become Christians after considerable mental and psychological turmoil. James' examples are of less interest to missiologists than our next writer's, in so far as they are examples of those in a Christian culture 'coming alive' to the Christian message after many generations of a society's exposure to it, rather than a transfer of allegiance from an alternative cultural and religious *weltanschauung*.

James defines conversion in a frequently quoted sentence: 'To be converted, to be regenerated, to receive grace, to experience religion, to gain assurance are so many phrases which describe the process, gradual or sudden, by which a self hitherto divided and consciously wrong and unhappy, becomes unified and consciously right, superior and happy, in consequence of its firmer hold upon religious realities.'[84] In commenting on this, E. Stanley Jones was closer to our original definition in changing the last phrase from 'religious realities' to 'a Person': 'the religious realities are a Person' and the 'divided life is 'unified' around a new centre – Christ.'[85] The aspect of the divided self, to which James devoted his eighth lecture, will recur later: he pointed to Augustine, Bunyan and Tolstoy as examples. This unification of the self 'may come gradually or it may occur abruptly…however it comes it brings a characteristic sort of relief…Happiness! Happiness! Religion is only one of the ways in which individuals gain that gift. Easily, peacefully and successfully it often transforms the most intolerable misery into the profoundest and most enduring

---

[83] T.H.L. Parker, 'Conversion', in: A. Richardson (ed.), (London: SCM Press, 1982) op. cit., p. 75.
[84] W. James, op. cit., p189.
[85] E. Stanley Jones, *Conversion,* (London: Hodder & Stoughton, 1960) p. 47.

happiness.'[86] Tolstoy is given as the example of a gradual return over the years to the faith of his childhood but his experience gave renewed 'energy' (Tolstoy's choice of word) in common with other experiences recorded by James.[87] James wrote: 'the personality is changed, the man is born again' and there is a 'new level of spiritual vitality...the new energies.'[88] He gives also examples of sudden conversions, those of the eighteenth century Christian Henry Alline of Boston and the nineteenth century French Jew from Paris, Alphonse Ratisbonne, and others to show what a 'real, definite and memorable experience and event a sudden conversion can be,' one in which often the subject seems to be 'a passive spectator...of an astounding process performed upon him from above.'[89]

James does not only use 'above' language himself. He recognised that much of conversion may be subliminal: 'the notion of a subliminal self' ought not either to 'exclude all notion of a higher penetration. If there be higher powers able to impress us they may get access to us only through the subliminal door.'[90] Like our next writer, James was aware of the often strange accompaniments to both conversion and revival, the influence of dreams and what one of the authorities he quotes refers to as 'the possession of an active subliminal self.'[91] James concludes on this aspect: 'if the grace of God miraculously operates, it probably operates through the subliminal door.'[92]

James realised that psychology, of itself, is unable to give an account of the source of conversion or even why those aims which have primarily been peripheral become for the subject, in his phrase, 'the habitual centre of his personal energy.'[93] He himself leaves the door open to a spiritual interpretation in a conclusion

---

[86] W. James, op. cit., p. 175.
[87] Ibid., p. 185.
[88] Ibid., p. 241.
[89] Ibid., pp. 225, 226.
[90] Ibid., p. 243.
[91] Ibid., pp. 240-241.
[92] Ibid., p. 270.
[93] Ibid., p. 196.

which may owe something to his father's Swedenborgian views: 'The visible world is part of a more spiritual, from which it draws its chief significance' and 'union or harmonious relation with that higher universe is our true end.'[94] He also recognised that, for the convert or mystic, their experiences can be 'absolutely authoritative in the individuals to whom they come.'[95] To take one prominent twentieth century Christian, well known to missiologists, who confessed himself sorry for the 'once born' of William James' classification, Stephen Neill: 'For those who can look back on some recognisable experience of conversion in their own lives this is so much more important than anything else that they find it very difficult to take seriously any type of Christian living from which this experience is eliminated' and again 'I have not the smallest doubt that through conversion I became a new man in Christ and that it was literally true that all things became new in Him.'[96]

II. Raoul Allier

The second of our twentieth-century authorities on conversion is of great interest to students of mission. Raoul Allier, who wrote as a professor in the University of Paris, published his *La Psychologie de la conversion chez les peuples non-civilisés* in 1925. He wrote in his preface that it was during a previous project on moral evil that he stumbled on the periodical of the *Société des Missions de Paris* called the *Journal des Missions Évangéliques*. This discovery in 1888 fired his imagination with the potential of missionary accounts for an exploration of conversion. In addition to the journal mentioned, he used a number of others, including the *Bulletin de la Mission Romande* (the Swiss mission) and the *Journal de l'Unité des Frères* (Moravian). He came, he wrote, to the whole study 'entirely disinterested' and had originally intended to include Roman Catholic missions but decided that the differences of operation were such that it would be better limit

---

94 Ibid., p. 486.
95 Ibid., p. 422.
96 S.C. Neill, 'Conversion', in: *Scottish Journal of theology* vol. 3, no. 4 (December 1950) p. 352; autobiographical MS, pp. 60-61; *Scottish Journal of Theology* vol. 1, no. 1 (June 1948) p. 95.

himself to Protestants.[97] Nevertheless, his examples came from a very wide range of fields including Madagascar, New Guinea, Greenland, Central and East Africa, the New Hebrides, Tahiti and Fiji. He used the printed reports of the great missionaries of the Paris Evangelical Mission extensively in François Coillard, Maurice Leenhardt and Hermann Dieterlen and the equally great missionary and renowned anthropologist, Henri Junod of the Swiss Romande mission, but did not confine himself to French sources and accounts from Johannes Warneck among the Bataks and a CMS missionary like Richard Taylor among the Maori also feature. He was acquainted with the anthropological writings of Lévy-Bruhl and with the psychology of Sigmund Freud, including his work on dreams. The work was in two volumes, the first of which divided into parts, 'Les prodromes de la crise' and 'La crise' – *prodromes* appears to originate with the Greek and Latin words (*prodromos, - us*) for a north-east wind which promised a change in weather conditions and can perhaps be translated 'stirrings' or 'winds of change.' His second volume, which will not be handled here, was entitled 'Les consequences de la crise' and the whole, with its treatment of over a thousand pages, must rank as one of the most extensive enquiries into conversion ever undertaken.

In the first part of volume one, Allier shows how resistant to conversion many individuals could be. One chief tells Coillard, 'the law of God is hard, difficult' and another tells a Moravian missionary in Greenland, 'we could have no objection to conversion if it were not so difficult.' King Sekhome of the Mangorato tribe told the Scottish missionary Mackenzie: 'For me to accept the way of God is as if I wished alone to attack…all the hordes of the Matabele.'[98] Debased and debauched habits cause a Tahitian to describe himself as 'in chains,' language, writes Allier, 'which is universal' for describing moral experience.[99] There is a clear recognition that the issue of conversion lies in the realm of

---

97 R. Allier, *La psychologie de la conversion chez les peuples non-civilisés*, (Paris: Payot, 1925) p. 15.
98 Ibid., pp. 131-132. Translation from the French is writer's throughout.
99 Ibid., p. 149.

the will: a chief asks Johannes Warneck: 'Where will I find riches and power if I never make war nor have slaves?'[100] Maurice Leenhardt produced a new slant on this resistance, what Allier calls 'endurcissement' or hardening against change: he found that it was possible to judge the spiritual position of his hearers by the allure of horses as a means of physical escape from the demands of his message: in one case, a man took himself off at a gallop, in another he retreated to another part of the same valley which had not yet been Christianised.[101] Malagasy parents went to the extent of hiding their infants in 'silos' to escape missionary detection. One African spoke for many in the various fields when he said to the missionary: 'You speak well but my heart is not ready'; or, with a touching faith in the missionary's prayers, as one of Warneck's hearers: 'You ask God who is perhaps able to change me; I am not yet ready.'[102]

As with William James' accounts, there is pain, or what Allier calls 'visible sorrow', before conversion: one woman, Mapati, reported on by Hermann Dieterlen moves from tears to joy.[103] The occurrence of pain and even illness prior to conversion causes Allier to compare the phenomenon with stories of Huguenots in the seventeenth century who became ill after renouncing their allegiance under political pressure. Allier judged that the deep distress before conversion was made up both of the *pain of converting* and, quite as much, of the pain *of not converting*: there was both the sense of an *obligation to change* and a *sense of responsibility for being in a permanent state which was condemned*.[104] He compared it to Paul's heartfelt expression of Romans 7:19-23. What is at issue is a new 'I', a new identity. In a section which entitles 'The two me's' he finds universal use of the language of the 'two hearts' by Maoris, New Caledonian Kanaks and Zambezi Africans. Moshesh, the Lesotho chief, said to Robert Moffat: 'Before I listened to you I had only one heart, now today I

---

100 Ibid., p. 141.
101 Ibid., pp. 201, 202 n. 2.
102 Ibid., pp. 203, 213.
103 Ibid., pp. 328-329.
104 Ibid., pp. 328-329, 330 n. 1.

have two.' Allier also gives an interesting example of subliminal factors at work: an African under the influence of chloroform speaks as if he was a Christian believer, although in waking life he is known not yet to be a Christian.[105] A Malagasy who appears to speak with the voice of the persecuting Queen Ranavalona I and associated ancestors gave evidence, as he did, that 'the old 'me' repulses what it sees as a menace.'[106]

This led Allier to devote an extensive section to the place of dreams as a factor in conversion, along with hallucinations and 'voices.' Of the first he wrote: 'the number of conversions provoked by dreams is incalculable.' Unlike western missionaries (but not unlike William James, as we have noticed) his subjects are not trained in mind to discount the power of a dream to provoke major change in life. Hermann Dieterlen, at first very reluctant to accept dreams as in any way a source of the divine, admitted that 'it is possible, it is not absolutely wrong': that is, God may have influenced the converts through dreams.[107] A typical example is of the chief who dreams that he is in the forest and wishes that Christians should pray for him to dispose of his fetishes: this chief, Kasi Ahang of Akropong, was so moved by his dream that he acted upon it.[108] Allier commented on this and other examples: 'It would appear that the moral will, vanquished during waking hours, takes its revenge during sleep: it is the new 'me' which emerges victorious.'[109] Reports of such dreams come from many fields, Kols, Malagasies, Kanaks, Africans from the Congo, Negroes from Surinam (Dutch Guyana).[110] In some cases dreams seem to have prepared the way for the acceptance of the gospel, as appears to have been the case in Nicaragua before the missionaries' arrival; or, less spectacularly, in Nias, where an elderly priestess believed that she had been instructed in a dream by the ancestors to

---

105 Ibid., pp. 365-366, 351.
106 Ibid., p. 364.
107 Ibid., pp. 373-374, 374 n. 2.
108 Ibid., pp. 380-381.
109 Ibid., p. 377.
110 Ibid., p.374.

pronounce in favour of the new religion.[111] We shall return to the place of dreams in the conclusion of this paper.

Allier's treatment of the experience of conversion itself, 'La Crise,' makes reference early on to William James. Like James, Allier described conversion as a new release but also as a form death to reach that point.[112] The call, as given by the missionary, Withney, to the Malagasies, was 'to abandon yourselves': but such self-abandonment, Allier recognised, was 'in a certain sense a form of death.'[113] One Malagasy convert, at first powerless to respond to such a call, then described himself: 'I feel myself as revived from the dead.'[114] Henri Junod had noticed how often converts used the formula 'I have been conquered' in the account of their experience.

For Allier, it was a clear case of the old 'I' having been overcome.[115] He concluded that, to say that birth was preceded by death was less correct than to say that both experiences coincided or 'arrived at the same instant,' and that this was true whether it was a case of gradual or sudden conversion. In both cases, it is manifestly real because of the 'new orientation of deep emotions' and 'changes of tastes and aversions.'[116] As conversion is a re-direction of the entire being there is no difference of essential nature between sudden and gradual conversions, though there may be differences of degree.[117] Even in those cases where conversion is a collective phenomenon, a scholar like Lévy-Bruhl had recognised that conversion is incomplete, unless it includes the conversion of the individual.[118] Like William James, Allier realised that the experience was authoritative to the individual: 'In the hour of conversion it presents itself as a dawning of the truth,' while 'the ideas…acquire a new power of realisation.'[119] We may close

---

[111] Ibid., p. 370.
[112] W. James, op.cit., p. 177; R. Allier, op. cit., p. 435.
[113] R. Allier, op. cit., p. 435.
[114] Ibid.
[115] Ibid., p. 436.
[116] Ibid., p. 531.
[117] Ibid., pp. 548-549.
[118] Ibid., p. 558 n. 2.
[119] Ibid., p. 525.

this treatment of Allier's work with his handling of the place of the mind and the will in a phenomenon which by-passes the intellectual…it is neither an action of the will nor…of the intelligence…we have seen how it forms a new 'me'. Is not this the matter (of importance) the transposition of values, the emotional and intellectual aspect of this transformation – are not these simply the necessary concomitants of the appearance of this new 'me'? The essence of conversion is neither an excess of tears nor adherence to a formula: is it not rebirth?'[120]

It is often difficult to know whether one writer has influenced another but before leaving Allier it is interesting to notice how closely the analysis of conversion given by the English historian A.D. Nock in his study of *Conversion: Old and New in Religion from Alexander the Great to Augustine of Hippo* of 1933 was to Allier's. In his preface and first of his lectures given at Trinity College, Dublin and at Harvard he wrote: 'As a manifestation both of group solidarity and emergent individualism, it is a sociological phenomenon of the first importance…impulses which lie below the level of consciousness and producing a delicate interplay between this and the intellect.'[121] By conversion 'we mean the reorientation of the soul of an individual, his deliberate turning from an earlier piety for another, a turning which implies a consciousness that a great change is involved, that the old way was wrong and the new is right.'[122]

III. Lewis Rambo

To read Lewis Rambo's study *Understanding Religious Conversion* of 1993 is to become aware of the intensive concentration of the social sciences and psychology on the phenomenon in the years since James and Allier wrote their accounts. Since 1980 alone, Rambo is able to point to some fifteen articles on conversion in learned journals of these disciplines and

---

120 Ibid., p. 526.
121 A.D. Nock, *Conversion: Old and New in Religion from Alexander the Great to Augustine of Hippo,* (Oxford: Clarendon Press, 1993) p. vii.
122 Ibid., p. 7.

this apart from the large theological and missiological output. Rambo, who himself experienced conversion and admits himself to be on a voyage of self-discovery on the subject, like Allier before him, discovered in the field of mission studies a welcome resource for his work: 'Forays into cultural anthropology unveiled an existing discipline that provided new insights into the conversion process...subsequently I discovered missiology, a field of scholarship initiated by missionaries working in cross-cultural settings that confront them daily with the complexities of interwoven religious, cultural and societal issues affecting and effecting change.'[123]

Rambo has regarded conversion as a radical experience in the precise sense of 'striking at the root of the human predicament,' a route which he described as 'a vortex of vulnerability.'[124] He showed himself to share some of William James' pragmatism, when he wrote: 'Stated starkly, conversion is what a faith group says it is,' though this definition, applied here to sectarian groups, can be inclusive presumably of the early church's emphasis on conversion to Christ, with which this paper began. He appealed to A.D. Nock, who had also emphasised the radical nature of conversion in the prophetic religions of Judaism and Christianity and by contrast to pagan religion in the ancient world.[125]

Rambo presents a seven-stage sequential model of conversion consisting of context, crisis, quest, encounter, interaction, commitment and consequences.[126] Missiologists have generally urged attention to context. Rambo holds that the context 'shapes the nature, structure and process of conversion' and that conversion takes place 'in a dynamic context.'[127] For Western Christianity this has sobering implications in Rambo's view. Religion is in decline and (following Berger) is relegated to the

---

[123] L. Rambo, *Understanding Religious Conversion*, (New Haven, CT.: Yale UP. 19993) p. xi
[124] Ibid., p. xii.
[125] Ibid., p. 5; cf. pp. 34-35.
[126] Ibid., p. 17.
[127] Ibid., p. 20.

private realm, while a 'unified religious view seems less plausible.'[128] Rambo guesses that in such a context parents will have more difficulty in retaining their children within the faith; and, further, that a declining religion will proselytise (his use of word) less.[129] Looking at non-Western societies he notices that certain social scientists see people as active agents of social change and he specifies missionaries as such agents.[130] He wrote: 'In many instances missionaries were rather remarkable people who fought for the welfare of the nations and sought to save them in an altruistic manner.'[131] In terms of conversions, so much depended in his view on 'the 'right' potential convert coming into contact, in the proper circumstances at the proper time, with the 'right' advocate and religious option. Trajections of potential converts and available advocates do not often meet in such a way that the process can germinate, take root and flourish.'[132] Such an analysis is borne out by, for instance, the conversion of the Japanese leader Kagawa, and the American missionaries who met him at his point of need,[133] as with many others. Relationships of this kind are central to conversion experiences for Rambo: he instances the personal influence of C.S. Lewis on Sheldon Vanauken, author of *A Severe Mercy*, or of the Christian industrialist Tom Phillips on Charles Colson as evidenced in Colson's *Born Again*.[134] Like both James and Allier, he identified the element of self-abandonment, whereby a confession of helplessness and an inability to care for the self (as, for example, in many participants in Alcoholics Anonymous) paradoxically begins the road back.[135] Again, like the earlier writers, he discerns that energy is released, previously devoted to an inner conflict now resolved, and becomes 'available for new life.'[136]

---

128 Ibid., p. 28.
129 Ibid., p. 34.
130 Ibid., p. 56.
131 Ibid., p. 69.
132 Ibid., p. 87.
133 W. Axling, *Kagawa,* (London: SCM Press, 1932) pp. 11-39; C. Davey, *Kagawa of Japan,* (London: Lutterworth Press, 1960) pp. 1-17.
134 L. Rambo, op. cit., p. 135.
135 Ibid.
136 Ibid., pp. 25-26.

If we revert to our original threefold definition of Christian conversion, Rambo gives little on conversion to Christ, though he notes the case of Eldridge Cleaver, whose childhood image of Jesus re-emerged at his conversion 'as a symbol of healing and transformation';[137] perhaps this is assumed, as he moves in a Christian cultural context much as William James. More seriously, he seems to ignore almost wholly the aspect of conversion to community, symbolised for Christians by baptism as both a sign of new life and membership of Christ's church. He might reply that, as I have omitted Allier's second volume, dealing with the consequences of conversion, he is entitled to isolate what Allier calls 'the crisis.' Nevertheless, in one who gives so much space to the social context of conversion, it is surprising that so little is given to the social and communal aspect of the convert. When it comes to behaviour, however, Rambo does offer guidance: the convert has to move from irresponsible to responsible behaviour and this includes intellectual responsibility in the refutation of false ideology. Ethically, the convert learns to transcend personal gratification and begins to live for justice in an 'other-directed' fashion, so that his conversion can be described as socio-political. Finally, he sees the test of conversion in whether it becomes an ongoing transformation: 'I would agree that people who convert and remain the same are not really on a path of transformation. They…relive the event over and over again but it has little power to transform their lives. Change is persistent and important and continuing and most religious traditions expect and foster change by providing ideology and techniques for the ongoing development and maturation of their members.'[138]

Conclusion

What does this review of three studies of the psychology of conversion tell us as students of mission? First, it gives evidence of the kind of inner tension involved for individuals personally addressed by the Christian message, what James calls 'the divided self' and Allier the 'two I's.' There is a deep and painful awareness of living in two contexts, of having 'two hearts,' a situation too

---

[137] Ibid., pp. 146-147, 202.
[138] Ibid., p. 163.

painful to continue without resolution. The resort, for example, to relief by way of galloping horse by Africans is an expression of the tension and pressure on the inner life. Secondly, there is clear evidence of how much of this struggle goes on subliminally. The example of the man under chloroform is particularly instructive. To say this is not to invite the Christian persuaders to adopt subliminal approaches, a method at odds with a proper respect for the human intellect and will: but it may lead, for example, to a reassessment by Western Christians of the place of dreams in conversion. A Judaeo-Christian tradition which, in its source documents, contains decisive dreams in the Joseph saga and in the early spread of Christianity, as in the case of Paul at a turning point of his missionary activity,[139] may have to be open, like the missionary Hermann Dieterlen, to the reassessment of the dream world: was William James right that the subliminal door may at times be the route by which external influence is brought to bear? Most primal settings in Africa and elsewhere sit more easily with the accounts of dreams in the Old and New Testaments than do modern Westerners.

Again the radical nature of conversion in the loss of one identity and the development of a new one described by the writers in terms of death and life, should bring home the profound issue at stake in all Christian mission. To quote Stephen Neill: 'What is it that has died? It is I myself. It is the self which, in its pride, has organised itself in independence of God and in rebellion against him. And does it want to die? It clings to life with the fury of despair. It is prepared to go to any length, to make any kind of compromise with God, if only it may be let off dying. That is why it is so hard to be converted; that is why we must never lightly use the expression 'faith in Christ'.'[140] The same writer reminds us, in calling for a modern William James, that far from being an adolescent phenomenon alone (a position William James also opposed) many well-known figures of the modern Christian world

---

[139] Gn 37:2-11, 40:7-23, 41:1-37; Ac 16:9. Loisy, Haenchen, Rackham and Lampe all consider Paul's 'vision' of the Macedonian 'during the night' to have been a dream.
[140] S.C. Neill, *What is Man?*, (London: USCL, 1960) p. 41.

have been adult converts, including such intellectuals as Bulgakov, Berdayev, Maritain, Marcel, T.S. Eliot, C.S. Lewis, and the Cambridge classical teacher Martin Charlesworth, to whom A.D. Nock dedicated his work *Conversion*, and many others.[141]

Tension, subconscious struggles, discovery of a new identity by way of a form of dying: these factors underline the deeply radical nature of conversion as described by Rambo and the radical personal change which is at the heart of the Christian experience. It can well be asked: 'What is the justification for focusing on conversion in an international conference devoted to a Christian critique of the world economy? Perhaps, however, there is a connection. For in both cases, at the macro-and the micro-level, the Christian gospel calls for change. In Karl Barth's words on conversion 'when we convert and are renewed in the totality of our being, in and with a private responsibility we also accept a public responsibility.'[142] Like R.H. Tawney, the Christian economist at the Jerusalem Conference of 1928, I do not believe that in order to change society you have to change the hearts of men first;[143] but, in so far as the call to conversion is a call to action, as Lesslie Newbigin's definition suggested, to align a life with the new reality of the kingdom of God and so with the divine will for justice and love, means individual lives so surrendered may indeed contribute, and contribute importantly, to a changed world order, towards that cosmic transformation which the Christian believes to be God's intention.[144]

---

[141] S.C. Neill, in: *Expository Times* Vol. 89, no. 7 (April 1978) p. 207-208; W. James, op. cit., p. 12 note.
[142] K. Barth, *Church Dogmatics* IV/2 (Edinburgh: T&T Clark, 1960) p. 565.
[143] *Jerusalem Conference Report* Vol. V, (Jerusalem: IMC, 1928) pp. 164, 169; T. Yates, *Christian Mission in the Twentieth Century*, (Cambridge: CUP, 1994) pp. 68-69.
[144] This paper was first presented to the 9th International Congress of the International Association for Mission Studies in Buenos Aires in 1996; 'God and Mammon: Economies in Conflict' and was published in *Mission Studies*, Vol. XIII-I,I & 2, 25 & 26, 1996, pp. 306-319.

CHAPTER 4

ANGLICAN EVANGELICAL MISSIOLOGY 1922-1984

Introduction

This short paper constitutes a preliminary examination of certain emphases struck by the two leading exponents of missiology among Anglican evangelicals of the period, Bishop Stephen Neill, whose recent death has been a great loss, and Max Warren. Some justification is needed for a paper on missiology which is defined in terms of ecclesiology and, even more narrowly, in terms of a particular tradition within an ecclesiology. Perhaps I may be allowed to let Bishop Neill himself supply the defence. In his Bampton Lectures at Oxford, printed as *The Church and Christian Union* he wrote: 'The problem of mission cannot be discussed *in abstracto*; it becomes intelligible only as the mission of the Church. Given a satisfactory ecclesiology... the answer to all the main problems arising out of the Christian Mission should be ready to hand. Where no clear doctrine of the church is held it is not surprising that the missionary problems present themselves as insoluble'.[145] Both Neill and Warren were Anglicans in denominational allegiance and in ecclesiological perspective. They were members of a body which defined the visible church of Christ as 'a congregation of faithful men in which the pure Word of God is preached and the sacraments be duly administered according to Christ's ordinance' (*Book of Common Prayer*: Article 19). Both were also Anglican evangelical by inheritance and conviction.

In Max Warren's case, this evangelical inheritance is easily appreciated. As chief secretary of the Church Missionary Society (CMS), he was recognisably in a succession which stretched back through Henry Venn, CMS secretary in the high Victorian period (1841-72), to his father, John Venn, friend of William Wilberforce and, beyond that, to Henry Venn of the Evangelical Revival, friend of John Wesley and notable Anglican preacher (1725-97). Max

---

145 Neill, S.C. *The Church and Christian Union* (London: OUP, 1968), p. 319.

Warren himself wrote: 'I am an Evangelical. I have never felt under any constraint to apologise for that designation, one of great and lofty lineage, not least within our own Anglican communion'.[146] He himself was the son of a CMS missionary and had served as a CMS missionary in Northern Nigeria, albeit for a short time only. Bishop Neill was also the son of missionary parents, who, like Warren's, served in India. He had felt the deep disturbances in Anglican evangelical missionary circles in the early 1920s in his own family, when his father had identified with those who formed the Bible Churchmen's Missionary Society in the divisions of 1922/23. He can be found giving expression to his evangelical standpoint as a young man of twenty-two at the annual conference of Anglican evangelicals at Cheltenham in 1922. The editor of *The Churchman*, the Anglican evangelical journal commented:

Nothing could have been finer than the address of Mr Stephen Neill (Trinity College, Cambridge)... Mr Neill deeply moved the conference by his frank description of the apathy that he finds among his contemporaries, which he attributes to ... the (1914-18) war. He is convinced that immediate experience of Christ as our Saviour through belief in the Atonement is the greatest need of the age. Modern preachers do not preach with conviction and are disturbed by all kinds of ideas as to what criticism has discovered. Personal conversion is necessary if we are to preach conversion. Only one who has been redeemed by Christ and sanctified by the Holy Spirit can manifest the sainthood that must be shown to a world in search of reality.[147]

Conversion
Warren and Neill brought to their thinking on mission certain emphases. One of these was the need for conversion, stated by Neill at Cheltenham and spelled out by Warren as one of the characteristic 'notes' of an Anglican evangelical in both his *Sevenfold Secret* and in *What is an Evangelical?* Perhaps it is particularly appropriate that, at a conference devoted to 'Christian Mission and Human Transformation', this emphasis should be

---

[146] Warren, M.A.C. *The Sevenfold Secret* (London: SPCK, 1962), p. 1
[147] Neill, S.C. *The Churchman*, vol. 36, no. 1, (July 1922), pp. 224-225.

noticed. Here, their roots in evangelicalism of the revival are clear – as Owen Chadwick has written, 'Wesley discovered that unadorned gospel of atonement preached to labouring crowds converted on the instant'.[148]Certainly, conversion was a theme to which Bishop Neill returned during his life. As warden of Bishop's Theological Seminary in Tinnevelly, he wrote: 'Conversion is essentially self-giving: it is centred in God... the possibility of instantaneous conversion, that the worst sinner who turns to God through faith in Christ does at that moment receive pardon for all his sins and new life... It is more than the sacramental regeneration of baptism, in that it is the conscious acceptance of the will of God and therefore makes actual, though not necessarily consciously experienced, the supernatural operation of the Holy Ghost,'.[149]

In the post-war period, Neill wrote an impressive article on conversion in 1950 in the *Scottish Journal of Theology,*[150] and more recent conversation with him by the writer has underlined how centrally important he felt this subject to be and how neglected the stress upon it in modern international Christian circles, though we may note that an issue of the *International Review of Mission* was devoted to it in July 1983. In one of his last publications of 1984, he returned to the theme on the vexed question of the Jew and conversion, indicating his own difference of opinion with Reinhold Niebuhr on this subject and his sympathy with the view that to deny the opportunity of the Jew to 'convert' was in itself a form of anti-Semitism.[151] Both he and Warren were deeply committed to the method of dialogue in the modern religious pluralism of our day, a dialogue genuinely open to truth present in other religious traditions, where there was to be no covert attempt to convert the other but where witness must be borne to the distinctiveness of Jesus Christ as discovered by the

---

[148] Chadwick, O. *The Victorian Church* (Part 1) (London: Black, 1966), p. 5.
[149] Neill, S.C. 'The Forgiveness of Sins' in *The Churchman*, vol. 48, no. 3 (1934), pp. 179, 181.
[150] Neill, S.C. 'Conversion' in the *Scottish Journal of Theology*, vol. 3, no. 4 (1950), pp. 352-362.
[151] Neill, S.C. *Crises of Belief* (London: Hodder, 1984), p. 42 and note 9; cf. Neill *The Church and Christian Union* p. 179.

Christian as his contribution to the interreligious encounter. But as to the importance of conversion and its modern neglect Neill remained convinced to the end of his life.

As I turn to Max Warren to explore two further Anglican evangelical emphases in his missiology, it will be plain to those who know their writings that both of these aspects were fully shared by Stephen Neill. They are the stress on *history* and that noted above of the *uniqueness* or *distinctiveness of Christ*. Any concentration on Warren here should be balanced by reference to Neill's corpus and his recent essays in debates on the incarnation.[152] They were as much at one on the importance of these two subjects as on the first. A fuller treatment of Bishop Neill's writing on these two subjects must await the future.

History
Max Warren was a historian by background and predilection. He had won a scholarship to Jesus College, Cambridge in 1922 and he became Lightfoot Ecclesiastical History Scholar in 1926. The bent of his mind was strongly historical. Although at home with the abstract ideas of the theologian, and well able to deploy them with effect, he had a mind for detail and for the concrete and he read very widely in historical studies. This was particularly the case in works about the British Empire and its development, which bore so closely on his own work at CMS. Some of this reading can be discerned in his two sets of lectures to the Cambridge faculty of divinity, *The Missionary Movement from Britain in Modern History* (SCM, 1965) and *Social History and Christian Mission* (SCM, 1967). His access to the archives of CMS and his knowledge of the great nineteenth-century missionary leader, Henry Venn, and his papers, gave added depth to this special interest.

---

152 Green, M. (ed.) *The Truth of God Incarnate* (London: Hodder, 1977), pp. 58-70, 71-88.

Certain leading ideas on history, a subject which becomes more and more clearly of crucial importance to modern theology, can be set out here in a synthesis as governing Warren's approach. Because he came to history from the standpoint of the biblical interpreter of it, these ideas were biblical in basis. He was not unaware, with many moderns, of the special position of the interpreter. He wrote: 'The interpretation of events is as much an event of history as the events themselves ... ideas, as surely as economic needs, make history. The economic interpretation of history fails to establish itself just because it fails to allow for this truth'.[153] In this sense, Warren was technically an idealist as an interpreter of history. He saw that 'ideas *are* aggressive and they seek dominion'.[154] But his own distinctive ideas were drawn from the Bible and this meant that he saw God in control of all history. Any division of sacred from secular, or of church history from secular history, he deplored. God was in the whole. He was at one with another contemporary Anglican theologian, Alan Richardson, in a deep suspicion of the retreat from history by continental theologians in Europe, a retreat into 'sacred history' or 'saving history' (*Heilsgeschichte*) if that meant abstracting the history of the people of God from the general historical continuum. He was prepared to concede what John Baillie called 'directional events' in the biblical story, but only provided that there was 'no divorce... between these events and the rest of history... In a strictly limited sense these events can be held to constitute a "sacred history"'.[155]

One Roman Catholic scholar, who has researched Warren's writings, wrote of his approach to history that he 'demonstrates that Christianity is never to be regarded as a religious activity divorced from life'. He held that the Old Testament prophets had carried the 'continuing burden (of)... a tragic divorce between sacred and secular'.[156] He set out to find God's hand in all historical developments, not simply religious ones.

---

153 Warren, M.A.C. *The Calling of God* (London: Lutterworth, 1944), p. 2.
154 CMS Newsletter, no. 147, 1953.
155 Warren, M.A.C. *The Christian Mission* (London: SCM, 1951), p. 20.
156 Furey, F.E. *The Theology of Mission in the Writings of Max Warren*. (Unpublished Thesis: Louvain, 1974), p. 90 and note 39; cf.

Early in his series of CMS newsletters, Warren noted the 'vacuum' in the soul of China. After the communist takeover of 1948, he asked again and again whether the communist regime was to be seen as a Cyrus, or as Assyria, "the rod of my anger".[157] He returned frequently to certain key Old Testament passages (Isa. 10:5; 45:1-8; Jer. 25:9; Hab. 1:6). As vicar of Holy Trinity Church, Cambridge, in the war years he had been deeply impressed by the message of the prophets, notably Habakkuk, and its relevance to the times in which he lived and preached: 'Munich drove me back to the great prophets of the Old Testament,' he wrote. 'A brutal and utterly callous imperial power was threatening... his (Habakkuk's) own nation's survival... He expostulates with God. And God then leads him out into a new understanding of history'.[158] This was that the Chaldeans were being roused by the Lord in judgement. Was this, Warren asked after 1948, the way to understand the Chinese revolution, Mao, or even Stalin? If the Christian is to be 'consistent and (have) a biblical faith he will see Communism no less as one of such instruments and ... Stalin and Mao Tse-Tung as two of God's many 'servants'. But that recognition will not minimise the awareness '...that these men, like all God's servants, stand under the judgement of God'.[159] He quoted D.T. Niles with approval: 'Why cannot we see the power of God manipulating the events of the world even as the Old Testament historians discerned it? God used Constantine – that is no justification of Constantine: or if God used the British Empire is it in any sense derogatory of God?' He himself wrote: 'history has much to say of imperialism, not all of it bad' and God's hand for good, despite the ambiguities, was present in the *Pax Britannica* as in the *Pax Romana*.[160]

Warren M.A.C. *What is an Evangelical* (London: Church Bookroom Press, 1944), p. 37.

157 CMS Newsletter, no. 148, 1953.

158 Warren, M.A.C. *Crowded Canvas* (London: Hodder, 1974), p. 99. *Interpreting the Cross* (London: SCM, 1966), p. 48f.

159 CMS Newsletter, no. 128, 1951, p. 17.

160 CMS Newsletter, no. 139, 1952; cf. Warren, M.A.C. *Caesar the Beloved Enemy* (London: SCM, 1955), pp. 10, 28.

Central to all history stood the figure of Jesus, his life, death, and resurrection, but Warren emphasised that 'Jesus was no *avatar*, a sudden appearing... he came in the fulfilment of time ... the time has come (Mk. 1:14-15).' He was anxious to stress Christ's own awareness of standing within the broad sweep of a historical movement. He too saw his place in time. He saw history 'steadily and he saw it whole, sanctified by the presence and purposeful activity of God'. Jesus did not so much *bring* meaning to history as 'bring to full realisation a meaning which history already possessed'. To some continental theologians in Europe, he was held to have brought a welcome emphasis on eschatology to bear on Anglo-Saxon theology, for example, through his book *The Truth of Vision*. He was certainly aware of the importance of eschatology: 'History without eschatology is in the strictest sense without meaning',[161] but he himself disclaimed over much emphasis on this, preferring to judge that his greatest influence had been through the essentially historical perspective he brought to bear (Letter to P.G. Meiring, May 23, 1960: CMS Archives).

Warren disliked strongly the term 'church history', as leading again to the fatal dichotomy between the sacred and life. He exhorted the principals of the Anglican theological colleges on this subject in a paper of 1960, preferring the term 'the church in history'. To speak otherwise was to him to 'create a completely artificial distinction within the Church's own life and to distort its relation to mankind. I could wish that we might have as the title of this subject in the curriculum 'the Church in history'.'[162] Dr Haaramaki was probably correct in discerning a similarity in his understanding of history to that of Arnold Toynbee's philosophy of history, where the future belongs always with 'creative minorities', whether or not Warren explicitly stated this. For him, whether in church or state, there is need always for 'organs of initiative' and so for 'voluntary associations'. And this was as true of his appreciations of the welfare state, as Lord Beveridge had intended

---

161 Warren M.A.C. *The Uniqueness of Jesus Christ* (London: Highway Press, 1969), p. 6.
162 Warren M.A.C. *Perspectives in Mission* (London: Hodder, 1964), pp. 102f.

it to be in post-war Britain, as it was for the missionary work of the church. He himself early discerned the crucial importance of the 'Social Welfare State' for the future both at home and abroad. The church in the welfare state represented for him 'the voluntary principle and is its main guardian'.[163] Within the church, the missionary societies represented that same voluntary principle of initiative, flexibility, and spontaneity. *The urge to centralise and absorb them must be resisted at all costs.* This antipathy to centralising bureaucracy lay at the root of his well-chronicled resistance to the merger between the IMC and the WCC.[164] He wrote: 'The strength of a democratic community is the strength of its voluntary associations' and 'the voluntary association has a vital contribution to make to the life of the Church no less than the life of the State'.[165] Tidiness of organisation was *anathema* to him as so easily spelling 'the creeping paralysis of death'.[166]

In a famous phrase, Lessing wrote, 'The accidental truths of history can never become the proof of the necessary truths of reason'. Warren was unafraid of the particularities, even the smallest particularities of history and their relation to Christian truth. How much more significant was Judea to Babylon, for all the latter's contemporary size and importance.[167] When we have learned not to despise the day of small things, we have learned a proper attitude to history, 'for, if God (is) in the little things, then *a fortiori* he is to be discovered at work in the tumultuous events of life'. Like Jesus himself, the entrance of the Christian mission is always particular and we can only generalise about salvation because it has been particularised in time and place.[168] He was well

---

[163] Haaramaki, O. 'Max Warren in Missionaerinen Ekklesiologia'. (Unpublished thesis: Helsinki, 1982), p. 55; cf. CMS Newsletter, no. 32, 1942.
[164] Warren, M.A.C. 'The Uniqueness of Christ' in *Modern Churchman*, vol. 18, nos. 1 and 2, 1974, pp. 156ff; McGavran – Warren Correspondence in *Church Growth Bulletin*, vol. 11, no. 6, 1975, pp. 466ff.
[165] Warren, M.A.C. *East and West Review*, July, 1973.
[166] Warren, *The Christian Mission*, p. 76.
[167] CMS Newsletter, no. 128, 1951.
[168] Warren, *Interpreting the Cross*, p.48.

aware, in interreligious debate, how this set the Christian apart from, for example, an exponent of Hinduism like Dr. Radhakrishnan[169] for whom the historical nature of religious reality was of no significance. In his debate with John Hick, to which we shall turn shortly, he criticised what he felt to be the static approach adopted by Hick, in using concepts of comparative religion, which failed to give due account to the movement in history: 'Geography is fundamentally spatial in its thinking. History is concerned with movement. Geography locates a race, a view of life, a nexus of custom at the point A. History shows members of that race 'on the move''.[170]

For Warren the practice of history was a mental discipline of immense importance. It constituted 'a form of obedience', 'a structure of life', as it had for a prophet like Habakkuk. The great need of our generation was to acquire this outlook which gave meaning to history: 'For our storm-tossed generation it is the prophetic outlook that we need, the profound conviction we have to recover that history is not a tale full of sound and fury, signifying nothing but a record of the activity of God – and all this at the institutional as well as the personal level'.[171]

The Uniqueness of Christ

Warren's newsletters of the late 1950s had given space to the renaissance of the great religions of Buddhism (June 1956), Islam (October 1956), and Hinduism (November 1956 and January 1957). He expressed his debt to Kenneth Cragg's book *The Call of the Minaret* with its sensitive approach to men of other faith, here to Muslims, but applicable to others. He edited the *Christian Presence* series which contained similarly thoughtful approaches by George Appleton (Buddhists) and Cragg and J.V. Taylor (African religions) in the 1960s. As we have noted, Warren was fully committed to the method of dialogue. His approach was

---

[169] Stewart, W. *India's Religious Frontier* (London: SCM, 1964), p.15ff.
[170] Warren, 'The Uniqueness of Christ', p. 63.
[171] Warren, *Interpreting the Cross*, p. 51; cf. *The Christian Mission* p.12; Warren M.A.C. *The Day of the Preacher* (London: Mowbray, 1967), p. 44.

based on Christ's prior presence wherever the Christian might meet another. Not only had God left himself nowhere without witness, but Christ had gone before any proclamation of him. Here was a view of the universal Christ, cosmic in range, awaiting discovery, as much by the Christian's dialogue with the best in another's religious tradition as by the adherent of another faith. Such people he refused to define by what they were not: a person should be defined positively by what he was, not stigmatised as a non-Christian or a member of a non-Christian religion. 'The essential missionary task of the church in all ages is to unveil the Lord who is already there'.[172] 'The Christian is not to take Christ to some place from which he is absent but to go out into all the world to discover Christ there ... to uncover the unknown Christ'.[173]

In the 1970s John Hick proposed a 'Copernican revolution' in theology. It was necessary to place God at the centre of the religious cosmogony as the sun had been at the centre for Copernicus, replacing the geocentric universe of Ptolemy. Of the effect of this on Christianity Hick wrote; 'In its essence Christianity is the way of life and salvation which has its origin in the Christ event. It will continue as a way of salvation... the needed Copernican revolution... is when (there is) a shift from the dogma that Christianity is at the centre to the realisation that it is *God* who is at the centre and that all the religions of mankind, including our own... revolve round Him'. Hick also suggested that Jesus' incarnation should be viewed as the language of mythology and that a positive re-evaluation should be given to the use of impersonal language to express the sense of 'the infinite reality' of God.[174]

Here was a whole range of issues with which Warren felt compelled to grapple. F.W. Dillistone rightly regards his main

---

[172] Warren, *Crowded Canvas*, p. 136; cf. Warren M.A.C. *Challenge and Response* (London: SPCK, 1960), p. 66; *Perspectives in Mission*, pp. 21, 41, 82.
[173] Warren, 'The Uniqueness of Christ', p. 64.
[174] Hick, J. *God and the Universe of Faiths* (London: MacMillan, 1973), pp. 49, 131, 141.

treatment of these questions as one of the best things that he ever wrote. It can be found in the journal *Modern Churchman* of March 1974. In this article he quoted J.M. Creed, a Cambridge theologian of an earlier generation, to the effect that, whereas Christian theology did not need to claim that it contained all truth of religious value, it was committed to the view that 'in Christ it had found the deepest truth of God'. Not to do so was for the Church to lose itself.[175] From this point Warren argued that the uniqueness to which he was committed was essentially inclusive. Jesus' relationship to God as 'Abba', father, is distinctive, but in this relationship he is Man, inclusive Man, relating to God. He was prepared to accept the Copernican revolution where this means displacing the religion – Christianity – (*vide* Hick above) from the centre. For such a religion can easily degenerate into idolatry, and so invite God's judgement, as any other religion, a view familiar to readers of Barth or Hendrik Kraemer. He then made a move which was characteristic but vulnerable to Hick's response: 'I want to argue that Christianity being removed from the centre, the new centre is not a theological term – God – but an historical person, Jesus, in whom God is uniquely revealed'. He repudiated absolutely Hick's view of the incarnation, as was to be expected of one in whose position the historical Christ was of such importance: 'I do not for one moment believe that you can have a theology of religion in the 'Divine as non Personal' and then go on to take the Incarnation as being, strictly speaking, a theological way of speaking about an incommunicable mystery'. But to emphasise the incarnation was not to do so exclusively; if so, why did Jesus himself speak of those who 'will come from east and west and north and south and sit down in the kingdom?' He gave full recognition to authentic experience of God outside the Christian tradition. But it is still 'Christ who saves', known or unknown. The principle of life and death and life and again, implicit in other religions, is explicit in Christian faith.[176]

---

175 Warren, 'The Uniqueness of Christ', p. 59; Creed, J.M. *The Divinity of Christ* (Cambridge: CUP, 1938), p. 113.
176 Warren, 'The Uniqueness of Christ', p.63f.

Warren had here combined two threads, both present in the New Testament but usually separated in his own expositions. First, the special significance of a historical Christology, Jesus as the man among men who reveals God uniquely and, with this, the universal and cosmic Christ, the one through whom all authentic experience of God is mediated wherever it is found, and often unrecognised by the recipient. Hick accused him of a 'profound unclarity' in the attempt to replace God by the Jesus of history as a way of coming to terms with the proposed Copernican revolution. But Hick accepted that if Christ be thought of as the Universal Logos, then a Copernican revolution was still possible. In the interest of his own view, what Hick could not accept was the historical Jesus still at the centre.[177] Warren's reply was to write that he had come to the view that 'uniqueness' as a category, without very careful definition, did not express the truth of Christ. He preferred a 'saving distinctiveness', 'valid for all men': 'it is this which justifies Christians witnessing to this conviction before all men'. He quoted Michael Ramsay's phrase 'God is Christ-like and in Him is nothing un-Christ-like at all'; and he refers to Jesus as 'the most comprehensive model' (of God) presented to man's religious awareness.

Much else of value is found in this printed debate, notably his insistence, already noted, on a dynamic and historical view of the universe of faiths, which looks toward the future in movement, and a movement of *convergence*, in terms of the New Testament looking forward in hope to the one who is coming. What Wilfred Cantwell Smith has called 'Participation', the inter-penetration of religions, was in his mind, one suspects, as he wrote of civilisations needing to be 'mongrelised' in order to survive. The danger of Hick's method was to solidify into past categories of comparative religion, rather than to recognise that, in a world of increasingly one history 'there is a dynamic at work which makes for convergence'. As he was to write in *I Believe in the Great Commission* (1976), his last book, that religious convergence centred increasingly on the figure of Jesus. In the words of M.M.

---

177 Warren, 'The Uniqueness of Christ', p. 65f; Dillistone, F.W. *Into All the World* (London: Hodder, 1980), p. 239f.

Thomas, the Indian theologian, whom he quoted here: 'It is not ... the mystic Christ but the historical Jesus who has made the deepest impact upon Hinduism'.[178]

Conclusion

If there is a connecting thread which runs through these three missiological emphases, it may be the theme of particularity. In conversion, God deals with the individual in all his particular individuality and we may assume that, as every individual is unique, so every turning to God is similarly unique in certain of its features. History has about it, as Bishop Neill often pointed out, an irreducible element in that, once an event has happened, nothing can change it. Jesus Christ is not only unique as other members of the human species are unique, but also distinctive in that he conveys salvation as no other member of the race has done or can do. Both these writers were prepared to face the particularity of Christian faith and religion, undeterred by the many intellectuals of their own generation or before who found this particularity a scandal. For both the issue of truth was paramount here.

Perhaps in a conference devoted to Christian Mission and Human Transformation the last word should be allowed to Bishop Stephen Neill. In his article on conversion referred to above, he faced the issue for the missionary which again takes the form of particular over against the general:

Should he try to detach individuals from the mass of non-Christian society by means of personal conversion? Or should he try to penetrate the whole of non-Christian society with the gospel, in the hope of introducing a landslide later on? This has been for a very long time a matter for debate in missionary circles in India. The time has now come when a verdict has been pronounced by the course of Christian history. It seems to be clear that those who have gone on the first line, of aiming at producing converts, have won (in most cases) a small number of converts, but have penetrated society beyond the limits of the range of their immediate and effective action, whereas those who have followed the method of peaceful penetration have made no converts and have

---

[178] Warren M.A.C. *I Believe in the Great Commission* (London: Hodder, 1976), p. 168.

penetrated society far less deeply than those whose evangelistic purpose has been more direct ...Every Mass Movement on record has taken its start from intense personal conviction on the part of an individual ...Any progress of the group ... always can be traced back to the courage and initiative or an individual.[179]

Yet, as we have seen, Bishop Neill's was no individualist faith, for no one laid a greater stress on the importance of the church for missiology and Christian life. Like Warren, in the labels given to evangelicals in the late eighteenth century, he was both a 'Gospel-man' and a 'Church-man'. In this, too, the two great men were at one.

---

[179] Neill, 'Conversion', p. 360; cf. Neill S.C. *Salvation Tomorrow* (London: Lutterworth, 1976), p. 84. This paper was presented at the IAMS Conference, Harare, Zimbabwe of 1985 and was published in *Missiology*, Vol. 14, No. 2 (April 1986), pp. 147-57.

CHAPTER 5

MISSION PRAXIS: CMS, the Mau Mau, Cecil Bewes and the Fairn Commission 1952-1959

Cecil Bewes (1902-1993), whom I have selected as my 'Telling Life' in this cluster of papers, like Bishop Sundkler[180] was a missionary in East Africa. He had studied at Emmanuel College, Cambridge, where he read history and theology. Here he met, through their joint membership of the evangelical Christian Union (CICCU), Sylvia de Berry. She was an Open Scholar in History at Girton College, when few places were open to women at all and so her award was a rare distinction. After Cambridge, both made open offers to CMS, indicating a willingness to serve anywhere in the world but they were sent to adjoining stations in Kenya and their romance blossomed. They married at Kabete in 1931.[181]

It was a Kenya made famous by such writers as the Dane, Isaak Dinesen (Baroness Blixen), Elspeth Huxley and Beryl Markham, aviator and author. The world of the Europeans who came to Kenya after 1900 had a caste of characters which has claimed the attention of novelists, biographers and film makers: there were aristocrats like the formidable figure of Lord Delamere, innovative land-owner and politician, white hunters like Denys Finch Hatton,

---

[180] This paper was delivered as a contribution to the Bengt Sundkler Memorial Symposium in Uppsala, May 17-19, 2009 entitled 'Telling Lives in Africa: African biography, autobiography and life history'.
[181] G.H.G. Hewitt, *Problems of Success: a history of the Church Missionary Society 1910-1942*, (London, 1971) I, 138, 135: 'CMS in Kenya was fortunate in the recruits of the 1930's...Leonard Beecher (1930)...Cecil Bewes (1929)'. 'Bewes coming to work (in Kabete) in 1930 wrote of crowded congregations in the small church every Sunday with two or three hundred sitting outside and an average attendance of two hundred in the Sunday school' (p. 135). The de Berry family of five children gave three girls to the mission field in India (Pearl), Japan (Doris, a member of the Japan Evangelistic Band, who died young) and Kenya (Sylvia): their brother, Keith, became a well known Anglican clergyman and student evangelist, based for many years at St Aldate's Oxford.

also an aristocrat in background, philanderers like Lord Erroll, almost certainly shot by the cuckolded husband and baronet Delves Broughton, subjects of recent films like *White Mischief* and *Out of Africa*. The Bewes' experience of Kenya was very different in the 1930s: their mission stations were among the Kikuyu in Kabete (1929-34), Kabare (1934-7) and Weithaga (1937-43) the last of which, perched high with a view of the Aberdare mountains, Cecil Bewes described as 'surely…one of the loveliest mission stations in the world'.[182]

Cecil Bewes became a fluent Kikuyu speaker and a biblical translator. He spoke later of his debates with Jomo Kenyatta on 'Kikuyu Orthography'.[183] His long service in Kenya (1929-49) culminated in being archdeacon of the diocese of Mombasa and acting as secretary of the CMS mission in Kenya (1945-7) and general secretary of the African Church Council (1943-8). An attempt was made by Archbishop Geoffrey Fisher, when Archbishop of Canterbury, to make Bewes a bishop in East Africa: but by then his growing family needed education in England and Leonard Beecher, another fluent Kikuyu speaker, became the Bishop of Mombasa and later Archbishop of East Africa. Bewes, however, returned to a post perfectly adapted to his experience: as Africa Secretary of CMS he worked alongside Max Warren as general secretary, a title which meant for him, as for Henry Venn his great nineteenth century predecessor, effectively chief executive. The two men lived in nearby houses in Blackheath in London, worshipped at the same church, the husbands with a

---

[182] T.F.C. Bewes, *Kikuyu Conflict: Mau Mau and the Christian Witness* (London, 1953) p. 11. Hewitt, op.cit 'Missionaries held the key to the new situation created by colonialism. Certainly they stood apart from the settlers' community; and could be seen to do so' (I, p. 142).
[183] Photocopy of an interview with a Bexhill newspaper, *The Bexhill-on-Sea Observer* in 1975 kindly supplied by Prebendary R.T. Bewes OBE: 'I used to cross swords with him (Kenyatta) frequently. We used to argue a lot on Kikuyu orthography'. For Bewes as translator with Kikuyu informants R. Buijtenhuis, *Le Movement 'Mau Mau': une revolte paysanne et anti-coloniale en Afrique noire* (Paris, 1971) p. 36; for Kenyatta as Bible translator G. Arnold, *Kenyatta and the Politics of Kenya* (Nairobi, 1975) p. 16.

common academic background of history and theology, with wives who were both historians, all four Cambridge graduates.

Bewes' period of office at CMS (1949-59) coincided with Kenya's troubles. The framework for these was an African population of some 5 million, an Asian (largely Indian) population of 100,000 and a politically vocal and demanding European population of 50,000. Since the Europeans had entered the country after 1900 there had been determined attempts by them to dominate the political process, not least in denying political representation to the Indian population, often educated and articulate, let alone the Africans.[184] Winston Churchill, during his time as secretary of state for the colonies wrote *My African Journey*, with the comment that in Kenya all the Europeans were politicians.[185] Churchill's influence secured representation for the Indian community on the Legislative Council of 1909 but even then he realised that Africans were being denied in what, after all, was 'their Africa'.[186] By 1940 there were plainly educated and articulate African politicians: Jomo Kenyatta had published *Facing Mount Kenya* in 1938 and earlier in the 1920s Henry Thuku had campaigned for African rights over the hated *kipande* (whereby African workers had to have their finger prints recorded) and the Hut Tax. A government commission of 1929, in its Hilton-Young Report, had warned of serious troubles if Africans were not given adequate means of political expression – as students of mission, we should note the influential role that J.H. Oldham played as a member of this commission, one which was judged (in the face of considerable European resistance) to have set Kenya on the road to self-government under a 'common roll' franchise for the different races.[187]

---

[184] G. Bennett, *Kenya a Political History* (Nairobi, 1963), pp. 7ff.: opposition to Indians went back to 1902.
[185] W.S. Churchill, *My African Journey* (London, 1907): 'every white man in Nairobi is a politician and most of them leaders of parties' p. 21.
[186] Bennett, *op.cit.*, p. 27.
[187] Bennett, *op.cit.*, p. 67.

The deep grievance among Kikuyu was over land. In the 1930s Chief Koinange and others had gone to London to give evidence to the Morris-Carter land commission, arguing for a greater recognition of the land rights of the Kikuyu. Koinange was bitterly disappointed by what he and others felt to be a failure of British justice in the report that resulted. In the 1940s the grievances were exacerbated as the European settler farmers profited from war-time conditions: the landless resented alliances made between European landholders like Delamere and landed Africans like Koinange, which favoured the already prosperous. Whatever else lay at the roots of the Mau Mau, land, and its connection with prosperity, was fundamental.[188] In the words of Adrian Hastings: 'Mau Mau was a movement of tribal desperation, backed above all by the landless, the poor and the young'.[189] A further aggravating factor was the treatment of tenant labourers or 'squatters' who had provided European farmers with labour, some 100,000 of whom, all Kikuyu, were 're-patriated' between 1946-52 to areas like Kiambu, forcibly removed from European farms, leaving them 'understandably bitter and angry' and only too ready to make violent attacks on the property of prosperous white settlers.[190]

Kenyatta had returned to Kenya in 1947 after a fifteen year absence. Although the hated *kipande* requirements were rescinded in 1949/50 (Lord Delamere's successor as political leader of the Europeans, Cavendish Bentinck, advising acceptance of this)[191] there was still a revolutionary undercurrent among Africans, which even Kenyatta, known as 'the Reconciler', was finding it difficult to control. He admitted to the American writer, Negley Farson, that

---

[188] B. Berman and J. Lonsdale, *Unhappy Valley: conflict in Kenya and Africa* (London, 1992) II pp. 245, 326; J. Lonsdale in *OHBE* (Oxford, 2001) vol. 4, p. 537; Hewitt, *op.cit.*, I, pp. 165-7. Caroline Elkins, *Imperial Reckoning: the untold story of Britain's Gulag in Kenya* (East Peckham, Kent: Owl Books, 2005).
[189] A. Hastings, *A History of African Christianity 1950-1975* (Cambridge, 1979), p. 88.
[190] David Anderson, *Histories of the Hanged: Britain's dirty war in Kenya and the end of Empire* (London, 2005), p.28 cf. pp. 21-33 on land issues.
[191] Bennett, *op.cit.*, p. 123.

he himself was frightened of the so-called '40 Group' of younger activists, who may have issued threats to his life.[192] Kenyatta was persuaded to speak publicly against the Mau Mau in Nairobi in 1951, when he combined denunciation with some anti-European rhetoric. By then he had combined with the family of the disaffected chief, Koinange, who had been alienated by the Morris-Carter Commission, to form the teacher training college at Githunguri: here, although recent study absolves Kenyatta from European accusations of complicity with Mau Mau, there was political indoctrination toward African political aims. Kenyatta married a daughter of the Koinange household, as did Bishop Obadiah Kariuki, an admired friend of Cecil Bewes, as Bishop of Fort Hall.

Killings began in 1951. Oathing had begun in the KAU (Kenya African Union) after 1944 which has been described as a 'fateful decision'.[193] Kenyatta had supported oathing in loyalty to the KAU but now Mau Mau took the process of oaths much further, with oathing by stages involving a willingness to kill Europeans in company with other militants and with an explicitly anti-Christian stance. Killing of Christians in Nyeri in May 1952 and as they prepared for Christmas celebrations in December 1952 were shocking: but the prime source of anxiety in that year was the assassination of Chief Waruhiu, devout Christian, land owner and African supporter of the colonial government on his way back from a land tribunal on 7 October. It was widely felt that, if police and government could not protect so responsible a citizen as Waruhiu, nobody was safe. The somewhat *laisser-faire* later years of Sir Philip Mitchell as governor were succeeded by Sir Evelyn Baring. Baring startled the colonial office in London, used to bland assurances from Mitchell, with a request for immediate emergency powers, which came into effect on October 20th 1952. A reclusive European farmer, Eric Bowker, was murdered on his farm on October 27th, hacked to death in his bath and his two African

---

[192] Anderson, *op.cit.*, p. 36: this writer notes that the leading authority, John Lonsdale, denies the existence of such a group in *Unhappy Valley II* p. 428 n. 50; but radical and violent Kikuyu there were.
[193] Anderson, *op.cit.*, p. 38.

servants also killed. The murder shocked the European community and made a deep impression on Oliver Lyttelton, secretary of state for the colonies, who visited within days of the event.[194]

This was the background to Cecil Bewes' visit of January 1953. CMS had decided that a goodwill visit of support and encouragement to (especially) Kikuyu Christians under threat was necessary. He took with him a written message from the Archbishop of Canterbury, Geoffrey Fisher, a recorded message from Max Warren along with a message to Christian women from Sylvia Bewes. The archbishop wrote to Kikuyu Christians: 'terrible tribulations have fallen upon you; many of you have had to suffer grievously and some have died as faithful witnesses to the Christian duty of upholding law and order and rejecting the ways of violent men. The Church in Kenya has been tested in the fire of affliction...from England there goes up a constant volume of prayer to Almighty God that you may be upheld in all perils'.[195] Bewes' book of July 1953 is 'dedicated to the memory of those Kikuyu Christians who loved not their lives unto the death'. By then there were moving stories of Christians confronted by Mau Mau oathing, which involved participation in animal blood, declaring that they had 'shared in the precious blood of Jesus' and therefore could never 'partake of this pagan blood'.[196] Much of the strongest resistance to oaths came from those who had been influenced by the East African revival, the so called *balokole* (saved ones), so that Bishop Sundkler wrote in his *History of the Church in Africa*: 'it was out of the 'Revival Brethren' in Central Province that the main opposition to the Oath and to the violent

---

[194] Anderson, *op.cit.*, p. 89. Sir Evelyn Baring was the son of a great British proconsul, Lord Cromer; he had experience of India and of South Africa before appointment to Kenya. In general, his governorship has been praised, though it is conceded that he made mistakes, notably over Kenyatta: cf. art. by A.G. Clayton in the *Oxford Dictionary of National Biography* vol.3, pp. 827-9, which quotes his *Times* obituary (12 March 1973) 'he found (Kenya) a land of danger and left it a land of hope'.
[195] Bewes, *Kikuyu Conflict*, p. 5.
[196] Bewes, *op.cit.*, p. 55; E.M. Wiseman, *Kikuyu Martyrs* (London, 1958).

struggle against colonialism emerged. A significant number of both men and women who refused to 'drink the oath' were killed on the spot'[197]; but, as he wrote, these Christians equally refused to join colonial Home Guard units, who were often the source of retaliatory abuses: 'theirs was a difficult witness…harder (because) the basic aims of the freedom fighters in the forests were also those of the Christians. They also wanted to see an end to colonial rule; they were also concerned about land and political rights…but they were unwilling to use violence to achieve their ends.'[198]

Cecil Bewes corresponded with the secretary of state for the colonies, Oliver Lyttelton, during 1953. He had become aware of abuses perpetrated against suspects by the over-stretched and under-manned security services. In January 1953 he wrote to Baring, cataloguing incidents of abuse and torture.[199] He thanked Baring for the hospitality offered in the governor's home during his visit. Nevertheless, 'Baring was embarrassed to receive a letter from Canon Bewes, providing a long list of alleged tortures carried out by whites in the security services against members of his church'.[200] In his book, *Kikuyu Conflict* of 1953, he reported as an eye witness account 'I saw a hospital ward of inoffensive, yet badly injured, men; had they been beaten up by Mau Mau? No, they had been questioned by the police'.[201] A letter from his friend and admired educator, Carey Francis, headmaster of the Alliance High School, confirmed the picture: 'I have not lost a moment's sleep through worrying about the Mau Mau; I have lost many hours through worrying about the security services'.[202]

In their excellent early study on Mau Mau, Rosberg and Nottingham profile CMS as 'of the Church of England' with a history of links to the British establishment and 'its traditions of

---

[197]B. Sundkler, *History of the Church in Africa* (Cambridge, 2000), p. 899.
[198] *Idem.*
[199] Bewes to Baring 28January 1953 PRO CO 822/471
[200] Anderson, *op.cit.*, p. 309.
[201] Bewes, *op.cit.*, p. 56.
[202] C. Francis to Bewes 29 December 1954 CMS/OSD G 3A 5/6.

compromise'.[203] The links were certainly obvious in February 1953, when both Cecil Bewes and the Archbishop of Canterbury were given time by Oliver Lyttelton in the House of Commons. Access to the state however was used then and later to good prophetic effect. Lyttelton minuted that he liked Cecil Bewes personally and he pursued the issues raised with Kenya, eliciting a cable from Baring that he was issuing a directive to both police and security services warning of 'severe disciplinary actions' if inhuman methods came to light.[204] Bewes was to return to these assurances at the time of the Fairn Commission as we shall see.

From informants in Kenya, Bewes became aware of a further case of abuse later in the year. An African called Elijah Njeru, once a CMS teacher, a hunchback who had suffered from tuberculosis, was beaten by two European members of the security services to elicit information on Mau Mau and a cache of arms. He died from the beating. Bewes took the matter up with the governor. Missionary informants on the ground were divided as to whether Njeru was implicated in Mau Mau or not, though on balance (like many other Christians) it would appear he probably was. Nevertheless, Bewes and Lyttelton with him were outraged at the treatment and further by the leniency of the convictions: manslaughter was not upheld but 'assault causing actual bodily harm' resulted in fines of £100 and £50 over the death: there is a revealing note in the file in the national archive that by then it was nearly impossible to get a European jury to convict other whites of offences against Africans and to this degree Baring's letter that 'two members of the Kenya Regiment...have been tried and sentenced' to Bewes was a sign of grace: but David Anderson comments that action by the Kenyan authorities only resulted 'after Bewes had again raised a stink'.[205] Bewes also raised with Lyttelton, largely to spare his embarrassment publicly if it came to light, another shocking piece of evidence of abuse at Chuka, when

203 C.G. Rosberg and J. Nottingham, *The Myth of Mau Mau* (New York, 1966), p. 106.
204 Baring to Lyttelton 11 February 1953 PRO CO 822/471
205 Baring to Bewes 14 October 1953 CMS/OSD G 3A 5/6; Anderson, *op.cit.*, p. 310; PRO CO 822/471.

twenty Kikuyu were taken out and shot, largely loyalist but suspected of Mau Mau involvement, under the direction of a British officer, who was ultimately imprisoned for his part in the affair. Bewes urged the government through Lyttelton to make a public declaration on how this case was being handled, not least with a view to reassuring African opinion.[206]

The opportunities for abuses increased, partly through the activities of the so-called Home Guard, recruited to counter Mau Mau in the African population and through the very large numbers interned in detention centres, not least after General Erskine's Operation Anvil of April 1954, a large sweep intended to break up the power of Mau Mau in the Nairobi suburbs. Many thousands of Kikuyu, among them those loyal to the government and well-known and trusted by the Christian churches, were rounded up on flimsy evidence and categorised as 'white' (little danger); 'grey' or 'black', the last being committed Mau Mau. Between 1954-9 there were all too many miscarriages of justice (some corrected on appeal), false imprisonments of the innocent and torture. David Steel, Moderator of the Church of Scotland, became a bitter critic of the Kenyan government for what followed from Operation Anvil and Kenyatta himself was given a seven year term of imprisonment in 1953, again on flimsy evidence.[207]

Increasing unease in the British parliament was shared by CMS. The society published an account of Bewes' visit in February 1953 (CMS News no. 1) and a fourteen page pamphlet on *Mau Mau – what is it* in May 1953. CMS tried to offset outbursts like those of the retired South African bishop, Walter Carey, in his *Crisis in Kenya* of 1952 with its highly coloured views of Jomo Kenyatta as some kind of witch doctor, whose 'hypnotic eyes' swayed Africans into a mood of atrocities; but they also felt a responsibility to denounce government brutality as it occurred. Adrian Hastings commended their stance and its moderation: not only had they sent 'Canon Bewes...an old Kenyan hand' but also 'early in 1955 the

---

206 Memorandum towards an interview with Oliver Lyttelton; Bewes to Lyttelton 22nd October 1953 CMS/OSD G 3A 5/6.
207 Anderson, *op.cit.*, pp. 208-9; Bennett, *op.cit.*, p. 135.

CMS, which bravely took the lead in so much of this, published a manifesto *Kenya – time for action* calling for major changes in policy'.[208] As he noted, this caused a rift between the CMS high command and their sympathetic bishop on the ground, Leonard Beecher, once himself a CMS missionary, who now accused Max Warren of pressing too hard when much was being done behind the scenes by churchmen in Kenya; and Cecil Bewes of failing to consult when potentially inflammatory statements and pamphlets were in process. Bewes defended himself and Warren on grounds of timing and respect for the need for independence for the bishop from CMS actions.[209] Bewes was invited to broadcast on the BBC on 'The Church and Mau Mau in Kenya', which he did on February 11th, 1955. The waters were further muddied by the resignation of the chief of police, Colonel Young, in Kenya, taken in Britain as a further sign of the unsatisfactory nature of colonial government, but by Beecher and others in Kenya as less of a clear-cut case than outsiders made of it, though the signs are that they were right, although Young was unwilling to embarrass Baring and his colleagues by going public on his real reasons, which probably involved too great a tolerance of abuses by the security forces.[210]

Wider public disquiet was manifest through a group of Oxford dons making a petition to Lyttelton's successor, Alan Lennox Boyd, in 1955, a group which included I.T. Ramsey, then Nolloth Professor of Philosophy of Religion and later Bishop of Durham, the Pauline scholar D.E.H. Whiteley, Iris Murdoch philosophy don and novelist and led, in deputation to the minister, by the Dean of Christ Church, that being the minister's old college to which it was felt he might pay special attention! Archbishop Fisher visited Fort Hall in 1955, where by then Obadiah Kariuki, Kenyatta's brother-in-law, was bishop, while the Colonel Young affair gave fresh ammunition to critics of the government like Barbara Castle,

---

[208] Hastings, *op.cit.*, pp. 102-3.
[209] Beecher to Warren 23 October 1953 'Confidential'; Beecher to Bewes 31 January 1955; Bewes to Beecher 9 February 1955; Beecher to Nicholls 2 February 1955; CMS/OSD G 3A 5/6.
[210] BBC text CMS G3 A5/6/7; Anderson on Young, *op.cit.*, pp. 299-307.

prominent Labour politician, and Leslie Hale MP, who corresponded with Cecil Bewes on the issues.[211]

The final straw for opinion at home over the Kenya government's handling of the emergency came with the reports of what seemed like a legalised massacre in the detention centre at Hola in 1959. Here eleven Africans had been killed in what the security services claimed was a riot, their deaths accounted for in a far from satisfactory manner, which however was accepted by the authorities in Kenya including the governor. An extended debate in the House of Commons included two particularly brilliant speeches late on 27 July 1959, first by Barbara Castle for the opposition but later by Enoch Powell from the government side, who, while commending Lennox Boyd warmly for his efforts in the colony, spoke devastatingly of 'a great administrative disaster'.[212] The appointment of a commission followed, consisting of R.D. Fairn, Sir George Beresford Stooke KCMG and Cecil Bewes: Fairn had experience of prison administration and of the West Indies as colonies, and the other two members represented the law and the missions: Cecil Bewes was the only Kikuyu speaker. His diary of the day to day work of the commission can be found in the CMS archive in Birmingham, hand written at the time, covering June 15 – July 7, 1959.

Bewes was pleased when his fellow commissioners responded warmly to his suggestion that they should begin each day with a short act of worship, Fairn being a Quaker leading two Anglicans. Bewes himself, on the first day, used the highly appropriate prayer attributed to the great English naval hero, Sir Francis Drake: 'Lord, when thou givest to thy servants to endeavour any great matter, grant us to know that it is not the beginning but the continuing of the same until it be thoroughly finished which yieldeth the true

211 CMS G3 A5/6/7.
212 Hansard Parliamentary Debates (House of Commons) Vol. 610 (1958-9) pp. 181-262; Barbara Castle (pp.219-31); Enoch Powell (pp. 232-8): a sign of the concern was the duration of the debate into the early hours of July 28, the two speeches being made at 12.32 am and 1.15 am.

glory, through him who for the finishing of thy work laid down his life for us, even Jesus Christ our Lord.' On June 18 they met a psychologist who confirmed the bad conditions at Hola and that Kikuyu teachers, however reformed, were not permitted to teach again, a source of deep resentment among an articulate group. On June 20th they met the Kenyan Minister for African Affairs, 'Monkey' Johnston, a man whom Bewes respected for his knowledge of Kenyan Africa: Johnston corrected them on teachers – given clearance by the Security Council and the Christian Council of Kenya, teachers *were* permitted to teach again. The same day Bewes visited his old station at Kabete and on Sunday he and Beresford Stooke went to Nairobi Cathedral, where he learned from a European informant that, having been invited to be an official 'visitor' to one of the camps in 1954 his offer to do so had not been taken up until 1958. The same informant accused the police of oppression, even of turning the whole country into a kind of 'Gestapo State'. On June 22nd a visit was made to Fort Hall: here Cecil Bewes noted the great increase in population from around 133,000 in 1933 to 350,000; and, with this, loyalist African anxieties about the return of Mau Mau supporters to their communities, one of them being Weithaga, his old and beautiful station. On June 23rd they visited the Aguthi camp at Nyeri, where detainees were divided into two compounds, that for the KKM (Kiama Kia Mungi), an association for the landless, with 369 interned, and Mau Mau supporters numbering 115. Bewes and Fairn (Beresford Stooke being ill) visited the Kandorga camp, where they felt that people were 'rotting' and the camp short staffed but they learned of innovative rehabilitation work by a certain Major Breckenbridge and his wife at the next camp, the Athi River Camp. This they found 'a most encouraging place', assured that staff never used violence, worried however by the use of darkened cells for confinement of offenders but commending the willingness to try new methods. After a visit to a women's prison on June 26, all of whom refused to speak to them, numbering some 1200, Bewes flew to the coast (Malindi) by then suffering from his heart and advised to fly after an ECG.

On June 28 they visited Hola itself. Here they found 600 detainees. There had been a hunger strike since May. The District

Commissioner, Tony Thompson, told them that his intention was to shift the emphasis at Hola from penal to its original intention of a camp for irrigation projects. According to African inmates, the régime had 'completely changed' since Thompson was in charge. They asked: 'can you keep him here?' On June 29th, the governor invited them to meet him urgently after their visit to Hola, about which they found good things to say but raised the case of one man on a seven year sentence who had been denied trial under the Emergency Regulations, a British version of the recent events in Guantanamo Bay and denial of basic human rights. On June 30th they visited the Manyani Camp, a camp with a bad reputation with 310 Mau Mau detainees: this, wrote Cecil Bewes, was by 'a long way the toughest place we have seen – but not nearly as tough as we expected': nevertheless, they noted a sense of hopelessness prevailing among staff and inmates alike. Another meeting with Baring followed on July 1st, fresh from consultation with the Prime Minister (Macmillan) and Lennox Boyd in London.

The commissioners began their report on July 2nd; but the same day they visited Senya Camp, where half of the Hola detainees were now held. None of the prisoners would speak to them, nor to the Red Cross or Fr. Whelan, an experienced RC priest and visitor. They discovered that the superintendent had sent out an order that there were to be no punishments until they had left: Bewes wrote 'that I'm afraid finished him. I imagine he will resign or retire quickly'. On July 4 a European informant gave evidence of torture by the use of an empty bucket being banged over the head of a participant and they received evidence that what had transpired at Hola was a well-publicised version of abuses dating back to 1957. Bewes did not accept all the criticism from Louis Leakey, famed archaeologist and Africanist, especially those directed at 'Monkey' Johnston, whom he continued to regard as very able with a deep and sound knowledge of the Kikuyu: 'is there a bit of personal jealousy there?' he mused.

As they prepared their report, Bewes wanted to include a paragraph which drew attention to the governor's assurances of

1953 against abuses, still found prevalent in 1958-9.[213] The other commissioners persuaded him that a direct attack on the Governor was only likely to alienate the British Government but all agreed that they should put their unease to Baring before they left. On July 7 they had a meeting with Baring, who, taxed with inertia, pointed to the difficulties, not least for the Police Special Branch who could bring suspects in at will, a practice easily abused. He undertook to take up reports of abuse with Catlin, Commissioner of Police. If Baring thought this would suffice, Fairn disabused him. Failures over five years on issues of torture were reiterated. Bewes felt that the governor was surprised by the uncompromising directness of them as a trio. The governor showed signs of taking the commissioners' ideas of a unified structure of command under the Minister for African Affairs to Lennox Boyd himself; but Fairn refused to permit this, as it must come from the report of the commissioners. Bewes commented at the end of the visit: 'we thank God for his many mercies to us over the last three weeks and pray that our visit will be of (help) to the perplexed people of a very beloved country'.[214]

John Casson gave a subtle and nuanced analysis, showing how Christian commentators easily fell into a 'binary' interpretation, in which they were no means alone, with 'African bestiality' (evil) against Christian (often European) practice (good), in many accounts conveniently ignoring the cruelty of the colonialism. Nevertheless, confronted by the bravery of Kikuyu Christians and their martyrdom and European and Africans murdered, a somewhat Manichean response was not too unexpected: the Revival brethren's response has continued to call forth the admiration of writers like Bengt Sundkler, and Adrian Hastings, apart from Cecil Bewes' *Kikuyu Conflict*, for their faithfulness unto death. Casson also raised a set of differing ecclesiologies: as far as CMS was concerned, with its roots in Continental pietism, there was a foot as ever in both camps: a revivalist ecclesiology of 'the saved', shared with the *balokole*, with its roots in conversionism and holiness, combined with the established church,

---

[213] Diary III, p. 17 CMS OSD G3 A/5/6.
[214] Diary CMS OSD G3 A5/6.

which in Cecil Bewes' case was used towards a prophetic stand despite a personal spirituality which drew on the Keswick movement and was again close to the revivalists. In a highly complex situation, some at least of the antagonism to the *balokole* by Mau Mau may have lain in their apolitical Christianity, where politics was viewed by the devout as a 'dirty game' from which one should withdraw, a feature of Christianity among Ugandans influenced by the revival that John V. Taylor had grappled with in his *Christianity and Politics in Africa* of 1957.[215]

In their report the Fairn Commissioners addressed what they had found and made a large number of recommendations, most of which the governor accepted in a separate dispatch to the Secretary of State, Lennox Boyd. They began by referring to the 'bestiality of the oathing ritual' and the martyrdoms among Kikuyu Christians, with the murder and mutilations of many 'peace loving people of all races' – we may note in passing that the total number of Europeans murdered was 32, while among Africans it was 1819.[216] They recognised the size of the problems confronting Kenyan authorities which involved in 1955 some 53,000 in 40 camps of whom 16,000 were Mau Mau convicts. They recognised also that, by a process of screening, some 78,000 Kikuyu had been approved as law abiding members of the population and that this was an achievement 'of which any country may justly be proud'. They held that natural justice required that detainees should know the reasons for their detention and they protested against the use of so-called 'shock' treatment, designed to secure cooperation (paras 43-79). They recommended that a psychologist with both skills in Kikuyu language and a Christian background be deployed toward rehabilitation, along with workers from both the Roman Catholic and Christian Council of Kenya communities. They commended Major Breckenbridge's methods at the Athi River camp and his

---

215 John Casson 'Missionaries, Mau Mau and the Christian Frontier' in P.N. Holtrop & H. McLeod (eds.) *Studies in Church History: Mission and Missionaries* Subsidiary, 13 (London, 2000), pp. 200-215; Berman and Lonsdale, *op.cit.*, II, 445-7 see reference to Bewes at note 75; J.V. Taylor, *Christianity and Politics in Africa* (London, 1957) pp. 18-9; *IBMR*, Vol. 30, no.3 (July 2006) pp. 153-6.
216 Buijtenhuis, *op.cit.*, p. 343.

'tutorial' system towards rehabilitation for wider implementation, though they did not approve of the use of darkened cells; and they opposed the use of corporal punishment elsewhere, which they found attested to by many inmates, though they were able to exempt Hola post-1958 (paras 59-61). The re-absorption of detainees to communities they realised to be a highly complex issue, subject to much manipulation: new re-settlement schemes were needed (para 65). They were strongly in favour of the use of detainee teachers and approved the separation of KKM members from Mau Mau, from whom they should be sharply distinguished. They wanted an upgraded Prison Training School: present inadequacies were putting off good potential recruits. They recognised that costs would be considerable but a necessary requirement: they did not underestimate the possibility of resort to renewed violence with Kikuyu problems still 'not yet sufficiently understood' (paras 88-9, 95). A scientific study was needed and they suggested that two social anthropologists (one being a woman), a social psychologist and a rural expert be used for this purpose.

Baring's response may perhaps fairly be described as grudgingly appreciative. He pointed to the difficulties in assessing detainees before an Advisory Board when witnesses were difficult to obtain and offering non-cooperation. He accepted the change of use for Hola from penal to irrigation schemes. He undertook that illegal use of violence would not be tolerated, re-absorption schemes were in train but on teachers he demurred: 'it cannot be too strongly emphasised that the Githunguri Teacher Training College and Kikuyu Independent Schools were to a large extent the *fons et origo* of Mau Mau. Some ex-detainee schoolmasters (might be employed) but others might do incalculable harm' – the commissioners had warned of deep resentment caused among a literate and articulate class by barring of teachers on inadequate grounds. Baring also differed on the KKM, which he held to be a revival of Mau Mau, willing to use 'violent means' to achieve their ends. Finally, he agreed with the continuing potential for violence but felt that there was no lack of knowledge of Kikuyu society and further study was not needed. Whatever impact his dispatch made on Lennox Boyd, the government in London accepted 52 out of the 53 recommendations contained in the Fairn report.[217]

Lennox Boyd did not long survive Fairn. Ian Macleod became Secretary of State for the colonies in November 1959 in Macmillan's government. Baring retired in 1959 and Macleod closed the detention camps, returning the final 1600 Kikuyu to their homes.[218] Macleod called a constitutional conference in Lancaster House in London in 1960 and included Jomo Kenyatta: the conference decided on majority rule and an open franchise. Kenya was set on course to be a multi-racial state with an African government, which became a reality in 1963 with Kenyatta as first African President. Cecil Bewes left the CMS secretariat in 1960 to become a parochial incumbent in Kent, where I had the privilege of assisting him. At this 50 year point of the work of the Fairn Commission of 1959 it may not be inappropriate to remember Cecil Bewes as one who laid some stepping stones to 'uhuru', as one who loved and supported the Kikuyu people and their churches and tried to maintain their human rights at a time of intense debate and some oppression. Like Bengt Sundkler, the well being of East Africa and its Christian population was a major factor in his life, as of Sylvia his wife and fellow missionary to Kenya. If, as John Lonsdale has written 'it was a rare Christian voice…and…took a significant amount of moral courage for Christian leaders to denounce state terror against Mau Mau'[219] it was just that moral courage that Cecil Bewes exemplified.

---

[217] Fairn Commission Report and Baring's dispatch can be found in the CMS archive CMS OSD G3 A5/6; *Church Times* obituary of Bewes of February 1993 for 52 recommendations.
[218] Anderson, *op.cit.*, p. 330.
[219] John Lonsdale et al 'The emerging pattern of church and state cooperation in Kenya' in Richard Gray et al (eds) *Christianity in Independent Africa*, pp. 267-9 quoted in Casson, *art.cit.*, p. 214. This paper was delivered at the memorial symposium for Bishop Bengt Sundkler in the University of Uppsala entitled 'Telling Lives in Africa' 17-19 May, 2009 and was published in *Swedish Missionary Themes* (Svensk Missions Tidskrift) Vol. 97, No. 4, 2009, pp. 541-555.

CHAPTER 6
NEWSLETTER THEOLOGY:
CMS NEWSLETTERS SINCE MAX WARREN, 1963-1985

Certain individuals in the world church are particularly well placed to listen to what 'the Spirit is saying to the churches' (Rev. 2:7). Among them in the second half of the twentieth century have been the general secretaries of the Anglican Church Missionary Society (CMS) in London, England. I have written elsewhere of Max Warren (general secretary, 1942-63),[220] now widely regarded as something of a prophet, with a vision that reached beyond his own time and place. Max did not begin the CMS newsletters (they were begun by his predecessor W.W. Cash), but it was Max who made them a vehicle for what he called a 'theology of attention', where he reflected profoundly on contemporary issues in the light of his wide ranging knowledge of history and theology. In his time the circulation of the letters was 14,000.

The aim of this article is to pick up the series of CMS Newsletters in the periods of Max's two successors: J.V. Taylor (1963-75) and Simon Barrington-Ward (1975-85). Although both, in their opening letters, looked back to Max as a 'giant',[221] each was equipped with similar, if also distinctive, gifts as a missiological interpreter. Both had studied Christian theology and taught it to others. Both had experience of Africa, Taylor largely in Uganda, where he had taught at Bishop Tucker Theological College, an Anglican seminary near Kampala, and Barrington-Ward in the University of Ibadan in Nigeria. Like Max, both had studied at Cambridge and came to theology from other academic disciplines, in Taylor's case English, in Ward's, history. Both had literary flair and skill, with the ability to encapsulate much in a brief quotation from a poet or a literary classic. Both were widely read and sensitive to contemporary writing and movements in the church

---

[220] T.E. Yates, 'Anglican Evangelical Missiology', *Missiology 14*, no. 2 (April 1986), pp. 147-57, and *Mission Studies* II-2, pp. 32-38; cf. 'Unhyphenated Evangelicalism: Max Warren, the Tradition and Theology of Mission', *Anvil* 2, no. 3, pp.231-245; *Supra* Ch. 4.
[221] No. 263 (September 1963), No. 388 (January 1975).

and its mission and proved able to reflect with insight on the church's essential task. Like Warren, they were aided in gaining a world vision by global travel and by extensive correspondence with Christians all over the world, especially in East and West Africa, the Middle East and the Sudan, India, Pakistan, and Japan – all traditional areas of CMS involvement.

The Years 1963-1975[222]

Taylor's period of office coincided with a time of radical social and political reappraisal. It included also such major missionary and world gatherings as the Commission on World Mission and Evangelism in Mexico (1963) and in Bangkok (1972), and the World Council of Churches (WCC) Uppsala meeting of 1968. It overlapped with what Taylor referred to as the 'shameful and futile Vietnam war,'[223] with the Cultural Revolution in China and, in the sphere of the missionary movement, with questions of identity for the missionary society and the missionary. Identity, Taylor was well aware, was a question faced by the twentieth-century-person-at-large: in a striking image he wrote of 'modern man peculiarly unconfirmed and uncommitted; like a hermit crab he has grown out of one shell and is scuttling around in terrifying nakedness looking for another. His most anxious question is 'Who am I?' and I sometimes think that it is the only remaining theological question which means anything to him.'[224]

Like Max Warren before him, Taylor was anxious to remind the Christian church of the wider context of God's activity in the world: on questions of church unity, for example, 'what matters supremely to God is neither the unity nor the holiness of the Church but the gathering together and the sanctification of

---

[222] A small selection of these Newsletters was published as *Change of Address* (Hodder & Stoughton, 1968). The title contains the *double entendre* of the CMS move of its headquarters from Salisbury Square to Waterloo Road, London, in Taylor's period 'incidentally' (p. 10), but the emphasis lies on the new approaches to an unchanging message.
[223] No. 301 (February 1967).
[224] No. 295 (July 1966).

mankind.'[225] He quoted another CMS (Africa) secretary with approval in February 1968, to the effect that

> the greatest single issue facing the Church in East Africa, as in the rest of the world, is the acceptance of the fact that God is active outside the structure of the Church and is calling the Church to be ready to abandon, if necessary, its entrenched position in its institutions and become involved more effectively in the life of the world. The Church is in danger of becoming a spectator, watching from the touchline the main arena in which the life of the world is being lived and where history is being made.[226]

Mission itself had to be seen more and more as the responsibility of local indigenous churches. Closing doors to expatriates could be the hand of God, 'the only way in which he can bring home to us...that everywhere the mission is the primary responsibility of Christians on the spot!'[227] In the context of WCC discussion of mission, Taylor was aware of the danger, voiced by statesmen like Stephen Neill and Lesslie Newbigin, that where everything is mission, easily nothing is mission: 'if we argue ourselves into a position in which 'mission' means everything that Christians may happen to do we find it means nothing at all. The missionary is called not simply to be part of the Church to which he goes but to be part of its outreach.'[228] He affirmed R.K. Orchard's dictum that missionaries should not be placed in the structures of the church but in secular life and in the structures of human society. In the aftermath of Uppsala 1968, he tried hard to mediate between the 'verticalists' and the 'horizonalists', as he called them: those who emphasised the salvation of God from sin and those who sought for change in human society and saw salvation corporately.[229] At Bangkok he voiced a rare and sharp criticism of the WCC and the National Council of Churches as he viewed the makeup of the conference in 1972: 'too few women...too many clergy...what

---

[225] No. 307 (September 1967).
[226] No. 313 (February 1968).
[227] No. 318 (July 1968).
[228] No. 279 (February 1965).
[229] No. 320 (October 1968).

was more serious, hardly any of them were parish priests. This fact, I fear, reflects the disdain of most National Christian Councils and of the WCC towards the life of the ordinary local congregation and its ministry.'[230]

From these general positions on the church and its mission, what follows is an inevitably selective series of issues, which stand out as especially significant to this reader in Taylor's set of Newsletters on the subjects of missionary cells ('base communities' as we have learned to call them), the approach to other faiths, the changing role of the missionary society, and such global issues as trade and aid and the Christian attitude to violence and revolution. These issues are by no means exhaustive. One is aware of much else of value that could be included.

Small Groups
Taylor and Barrington-Ward both laid heavy emphasis on the need for the world church to use the dynamic of small groups in mission. Taylor was writing in the period when E.F. Schumacher was influential: he quoted Schumacher twice approvingly. It was not, however, only in the world of economics that the two secretaries saw that 'small is beautiful.' Faced with large formal structures like the CWME meetings at Mexico, Taylor reflected on Gideon and his small band (Judges 7) as 'God's arithmetic'.[231] Small groups of Christians are variously described as 'little congregations,' whose 'close community' can turn the church once more into the healer of men's souls. Here is to be found the intimacy and the informality where 'the penetrating, forgiving love of the Gospel [can] get to work.'[232] Such groups, whether as African bush churches or as British house groups, need to be 'set free' by the local and larger congregations, to be 'responsible to God for the mission in their own situation,' for they are the real growing edges of the church in the modern world. The centre, however, will always be wary of giving them the freedom that they

---

[230] No. 370 (April 1973).
[231] No. 268 (February 1964).
[232] No. 277 (December 1964); cf. No. 299 (December 1966).

need.[233] To hold out for larger structures and claim that that larger units (like parishes in England) are not 'breaking down' is to ignore the fact that 'unhappily too many parish priests are, all over the world.'[234] J.H. Oldham was right to judge that 'if we need to make a thing real we must make it local.' For many outsiders, that local reality is best experienced in the small group, where one can belong without first being committed.[235] He noticed the release of human resources achieved in the Anglican Church of Uganda through the use of groups by a provincial training team, led, interestingly in the light of subsequent fame, by Terry Waite.[236] Such groups can become 'cells of defiance,' foci of alternative lifestyles. Such experiments as the kibbutz in Israel or the communities in the United States after the 'hippy revolution' taught this lesson: and Christian ashrams in India or Dilaram House in Kabul, founded in 1971 to pick up the casualties of the hippy trail in a 'house of the peaceful heart,'[237] gave evidence for it. Reflecting on such great twentieth-century Christians as C.S. Lewis, Florence Allshorn, and Max Warren himself, Taylor noted the importance of groups of Christian friends, here called 'coteries', in their development: 'if we want men of stature we should remember that they have always grown better in coteries of friends than in structures of efficiency.'[238] This continuing tension among the formal, the structured and the 'organisation' over against the small, the personal, and the spontaneous is noticeably common to both secretaries they grapple with the renewal of Christian life by the gospel in the second half of the twentieth century. The vital experience of the gospel, in its community manifestation, is for our day to be found in these cells of mission.

The Approach to Other Faiths
Here Taylor shared the basic approach of Max Warren and other contributors to the 'Christian Presence' series. He himself had

---

233 No. 299 (December 1966).
234 No.308 (October 1967).
235 No. 311 (December 1967).
236 No. 354 (November 1971).
237 No. 283 (July 1974).
238 No. 384 (September 1974).

written the volume on African religion in *The Primal Vision* (1963). He echoed it here in stating his conviction that 'the unceasing sense of this all-pervasive God was too much for African man and he sought to escape by elevating one of his ancestral heroes of the tribe and identifying him with...the far-off aspect of God [and so was] able to keep him at a safe distance.'[239] When the Yaoundé consultation tended to talk of the African sense of the 'High God', Taylor preferred 'a strong sense of the God-who-is-near.'[240] In regard to the great religious tradition of the East, Taylor had found many Hindus and some Muslims who were increasingly open to the gospel of Christ, while remaining within their own religious structures. Of Hindus he wrote: 'though they are at pains to show that his [Christ's] teachings were all anticipated in the Bhagavad Gita and the great epics, a steadily growing number...are prepared to admit to a deep devotion – that is not too strong a word – to the Lord Jesus Christ...many of the so-called 'secret Christians' today openly accept all the obligations of discipleship short of baptism'.[241]

There was evidence of a kind of Christian 'blood-transfusion' in Hinduism, symbolised for Taylor by the posters, displayed by Hindus in East Africa at the time of the death of Gandhi, which carried the representation of Christ's cross. Why, despite all the symbols available to so syncretist a tradition was this chosen above all? Taylor quoted Hans Küng with approval: 'the gospel of Jesus Christ is able to liberate the truth of the world religions from their entanglement in error or sin...what we believe in is *service* of the religions of the world by the Church of Jesus Christ, in love.' Taylor preferred the word 'exchange' to 'dialogue' to make the point that 'in all its dialogue and exchange with another religion the Church must desire, not to overcome and displace, but to redeem and be itself redeemed.'[242] The seeds of Taylor's later book on the Holy Spirit, *The Go-Between God* (1972), were present when he reminded that the Holy Spirit has been at work 'evoking

---

[239] No. 338 (May 1970).
[240] No. 287 (November 1965).
[241] No. 291 (March 1966).
[242] No. 328 (June 1969); No. 303 (April 1967).

the responses of that other faith and ceaselessly pointing to Christ': but any fulfilment will be the 'same devastating' way by which he fulfilled Judaism, 'by means of revolution rather than evolution'.[243] Taylor judged John Hick's approach to have failed because it did 'not take seriously enough the very distance and discontinuities – the lack of common ground and common speech,' what Roger Hooker, whom he quoted, stated as 'the real problem...that we cannot disagree, for disagreement assumes a common language.' The appeal to a timeless Christ was too easy a solution, for it begged the question 'whether [or not] the death and resurrection of Jesus added anything to the Word which was already spoken in other periods of history.'[244] The Christian can accept that God's redeeming activity is at work continually in the 'basic humanness' of others but his responsibility remains to pass on what in 'his moments of highest aspiration' he desires for himself: 'the privilege of walking consciously in the steps and the power of the Crucified. For in a universe of which he is Maker and the Lord the fullness of life cannot mean less than that.'[245] Taylor held firmly to the Christian responsibility to proclaim in these terms, maintaining the uniqueness and universality of Jesus Christ, but doing so always with sensitivity to the other, open to the Holy Spirit in him and in his tradition. The Christian should affirm pluralism as God's opportunity given for a new 'exchange' to happen.[246]

The Changing Role of the Missionary Society

In March 1967 Taylor quoted *Alice in Wonderland*: 'Who in the world am I? Ah, *that's* the greatest puzzle,' and with this Alice's reply to the caterpillar's question, 'Who are you?' – 'I hardly know, sir, just at present.' The missionary society was in transition.[247] There was an element of crisis of identity. For himself he wanted to revive the sense of movement over against institution, in a society that had become too much a part of the religious

---

243 No.330 (September 1969); No. 303 (April 1967).
244 No.379 (March 1974).
245 No. 330 (September 1969).
246 No. 303 (April 1967).
247 No. 302 (March 1967).

establishment.[248] This was the period of the growth of the short-term volunteer. While initially hesitant, Taylor came to see these offers as valid and to be welcomed. He recognised the mood of the 1960s when a young person could say only, 'I will go now: who knows what will happen next year?' But he emphasised that 'no Christian can ultimately discharge his obligations to the world by means of short projects.'[249] The CMS needed also to enlarge its vision and welcome 'associates', those who were not missionaries in the strict sense, serving with foreign governments in some secular role. There was a need for a 'brotherhood of commitment', which would include all those at home who supported the work, and even those of other denominational allegiance who were prepared to join the society. The same expectation of service would be laid on associates and missionaries by the society, both of whom would have 'absolutely equal standing…despite the different pay packets.'[250]

Like Warren and Henry Venn, Taylor stood by the essentially voluntary nature of the missionary society against any absorption into the structures of the church. He cited the case of de Nobili in India, who had done by individual initiative and flexibility what the Roman church corporately could not do.[251] He quoted the wry comments of the CMS president and leading Anglican layman, Sir Kenneth Grubb, that the Church of England might be a 'nice' body, but 'it does not strike me with irresistible force as an enterprising or an enthusiastic one, ready to spend and be spent in the world-wide extension of the kingdom of God.' Taylor saw the need for missionary societies, as also religious orders, to provide 'communities of missionary dedication' 'to hold their scattered members faithful to a common ideal.'[252]

---

[248] No. 285 (September 1965).
[249] No. 289 (January 1966).
[250] No.302 (March 1967).
[251] No.349 (May 1971).
[252] No. 370 (April 1973). The quotation from K. Grubb is in Grubb, *Crypts of Power* (London: Hodder & Stoughton, 1971), p. 154.

Global issues

On matters of trade and aid, Taylor called, early in his series, for 'drastic political action to bring about a guided international economy.'[253] With Professor S.L. Parmar, professor of economics at the University of Allahabad, he saw the need for 'a completely new concept of international economy wherein less developed nations would be treated in the same way that a nation treats its less developed areas.'[254] A 'global taxation' system was required out of 'gross national incomes to replace or augment our present laissez-faire aid, given or withheld on the political will of donor nations.'[255] Confronted by an increasingly strong emphasis on violence and revolution to attain social and political goals, Taylor stated the need to 'help members of our society' to 'free themselves from the deeply ingrained reaction against all who resort to violence' by the recognition of repressive regimes and their backing by the great powers, and the need to recognise '*God* as the great subversive agent on behalf of the poor and the dispossessed.'[256] Elijah's 'still small voice' had, in fact, been a divine instigation to topple political order by revolution.[257]

The Years 1975 – 1985

Simon Barrington-Ward shared many of John Taylor's concerns in his own series of Newsletters, not least the emphasis on missionary cells. He had also certain distinctive preoccupations. The contrasts between the macrocosmic and the microcosmic, of organisation against organism, of direction against freedom, of the cerebral against the spontaneous, of the intellect against the imagination, of the ideal against reality – these great antitheses and, still more, their resolution in Christ recur again and again. In two outstanding attempts to interpret the history of Mao's China,[258] he showed how Mao's original inspiration had been a grassroots revolution arising from the peasant farmer rather than from the Russian model based

---

253 No. 291 (March 1966).
254 No. 298 (November 1966).
255 No. 324 (February 1969).
256 No. 339 (June 1970).
257 No. 359 (April 1972).
258 Nos. 396, 397 (October 1975, November 1975).

on the urban middle class. Inevitably, however, an elite of administrators had imposed themselves on this ideal in the mid-1960s. Mao then sought to recover the original dynamic by means of the Cultural Revolution and its Red Guards, with experts banished to collective farms and intense group confessions providing new social energy. Nevertheless, China, like the church, found that it needed the 'Two Legs' – order, structure, and organisation *with* communal experience – if it were to advance.

A second overriding preoccupation, rooted in the gospel but with an admitted indebtedness to the philosopher John Macmurray,[259] was with the personal. It is the personal that is so easily lost in formal structures, in church organisation, by the 'system', even by theology itself in the hands of certain exponents. 'The undermining, the destruction of the union of Jesus himself with God, the taking apart of the Trinitarian heart of our faith is really an attempt to remove the very personal ground for which people everywhere are seeking. As St. Thomas [Aquinas] declared, speaking of the Trinity,' persona est relatio,' the personal consists in relatedness.'[260] Personal quality of life is an important aspect of mission seen in Mother Teresa, in whom a Hindu can recognise holiness of life,[261] in African itinerant preachers, who are remembered as carrying with them an inner stillness,[262] in a missionary like C.F. Andrews, who mediated to Gandhi and Tagore the possibility of a new relationship with Europeans.[263] Above all, Jesus himself is the 'unifying centre', 'the authentic touch of personal love restoring unity and coherence.' He becomes 'together with those who live 'in Him' the new source of fully personal life.[264] Hegel had been right to see in Jesus the resolution of the ideal and the real.[265]

---

[259] No. 391 (April 1975); No. 405 (October 1976); No. 436 (October 1980).
[260] No. 404 (September 1976).
[261] No. 398 (December 1975).
[262] No. 412 (September 1977).
[263] No. 439 (March 1981).
[264] No. 414 (December 1977).
[265] No. 468 (July 1985).

Nearly a quarter of this series (20 out of 83 letters) contain some reference to 'base communities', missionary cells, the way of realising this combination of the dynamic and the personal in Christian life. Barrington-Ward gave evidence that his own personal pilgrimage owed much to such a Christian group in post-war Berlin, neither Marxist nor 'free Western' in ideas, but open, accepting, vigorous.[266] In such groups, the 'gospel finds corporate and physical form', 'faith becomes active in love' (a favourite text), and local people are mobilised to meet the needs of the community and, in the process, find a fresh relevance in Bible study.[267] Enthusiastic as he was about such groups as a 'growing world-wide theme',[268] when espoused by Charles Elliot as 'the only answer' Barrington-Ward sounds a note of caution: 'small may be beautiful but small is not enough.'[269] As in China's experiment, both 'legs' are needed. He wrote in another context: 'the Bible gives us good grounds for sticking with the institutional church to the uttermost.'[270] Nevertheless, despite this caveat, it is to these base communities, Taylor's 'cells of defiance', that he looks for the renewal of the church's life, as manifested by Dilaram, which he, like Taylor, admired for its practical incarnation of Christian community and care; in lay theologising groups in Nigeria, associated with agricultural progress;[271] in groups in Hong Kong flats; in Aboriginal villages in Australia; in youth camps in Calcutta.[272]

On the issue of the approach to other faiths, Barrington-Ward, like his two predecessors, Warren and Taylor, takes issue with John Hick (and here Wilfred Cantwell Smith) over any attempt to treat religions as each a part of a common reality. There is indeed a need for a 'Copernican revolution', but it is a different one from Hick's. Muslims and Christians alike, with other so-called unified systems (which both Christendom and Islam have represented),

---

[266] No. 427 (July 1979).
[267] No. 395 (September 1975); No. 423 (January 1979).
[268] No. 394 (July 1975).
[269] No. 411 (July 1977).
[270] No. 461 (June 1984).
[271] No. 420 (September 1978); No. 423 (January 1979).
[272] No.435 (September 1980).

need to become aware that these are an illusion. Systems need to come to the cross to be broken and so discover a new personal reality.[273] He instanced one Muslim, who had become increasingly aware of a gap between head and heart, a condition Barrington-Ward had found present in varied settings: with an Australian Aborigine, an ambulance worker in his own London suburb, and an East African Nganga healer. For the gulf 'between intellect and imagination, reason and feeling,... [and for] an increasingly sharp discontinuity between ideal and hard reality...heaven and earth' found in these cases, Christ provided the bridge and the possibility of healing this schism, this 'tragic disintegration of an existence,' to make of it 'some ultimate whole.'[274]

In the final letter of the series, Barrington-Ward put on record his conviction that those Westerners who have converted to Islam, to Hinduism, or to African and Asian cults have been fleeing from the divisive effects of modernity on their culture into the 'alternative wholeness' offered. But this wholeness is an illusion. Those, however, who have moved in the other direction, out of the these faiths and toward Christ, have, in his experience, been those who

> 'again and again proved to be people who were actively seeking to grapple realistically, critically but also positively, with those divisions of modernity. They were genuinely trying to take hold of change, to accept and yet to resolve the conflict. They found in Christ crucified, in a way that Christians in the West are still often only beginning to find, 'one Mediator between God and human beings'...within a new secularised, humanised, vulnerable world'.[275]

Conclusion

If to listen to these voices is to catch the voice of the Spirit to modern missionary obedience, we should hear the importance to

---

[273] No.401 (March 1976).
[274] No.445 (January 1982).
[275] No. 471 (December 1985). This paper appeared in the *IBMR*, Vol. 12, No. 1. 1988, pp. 11-15.

our day of the 'base communities' as the incarnation of forgiving love with their potential for radical Christian energy and action, 'faith working through love.' There should be an openness to other religious traditions, with an eye for religious 'blood-transfusions' and an awareness of the breakdown of simplified unities. There should also be the integration of the formal and institutional with the small and dynamic in a personal unity shaped by the cross, where men and women are able to exhibit a deepened and integrated quality of life – in a frequent quotation, by Barrington-Ward of T.S. Eliot: ' to think their feelings and feel their thoughts.' These, at least, are some of the insistent themes for the theory and practice of world mission from these 207 essays in 'Newsletter theology'.

PART II

THINKERS

CHAPTER 7

STEPHEN NEILL: some aspects of a theological legacy – Conversion, the uniqueness of Christ, Christ and History

In an earlier article I tried to show how Max Warren and Stephen Neill belonged to a significant group of Anglican evangelicals, who stood between the conservatives and the liberals and preferred to be thought of as evangelicals without any prefix.[276] Since Stephen Neill's death we have had two general appreciations of his life and work, one from equally distinguished writers and fellow members of the British Academy as himself and a helpful general assessment from Christopher Lamb. We wait in hope for the publication of his autobiography.[277] Here the intention is to notice some of the theological and missiological inheritance left to us by a great scholar, writer, teacher and missionary.

Conversion
One of the themes to which Stephen Neill returned throughout his life and which he believed to be sadly neglected both in the Anglican world and in the context of the World Council of Churches was the Christian experience of conversion, and its significance. His autobiography reveals that he himself underwent a conversion experience as a school-boy at Dean Close School in

---

[276] T. E. Yates, 'Evangelicalism without Hyphens: Max Warren, the Tradition and Theology of Mission' *Anvil*, vol. 2, no. 3 (1985) pp. 231-245. Cf. the short appreciation of Stephen Neill in *Anvil*, vol. 1, no. 3 (1984) pp. 198-9; S. C. Neill, *Anglicanism*, pp. 400-401; *Supra* Ch. 4.

[277] A. K. Cragg and W. O. Chadwick, 'Stephen Charles Neill 1900-1984' in *Proceedings of the British Academy*, vol. LXXI (1985), pp. 603-614: this is available separately. Cf. 'Stephen Neill' *International Bulletin of Missionary Research*, vol. II, no. 2 (April 1987) pp. 62-66; *Mission Legacies* ed. G. H. Anderson, R. T. Coote, N. A. Horner, J. M. Phillips (New York: Orbis, 1994) pp. 445-51 (C. Lamb). The autobiography appeared in 1991 as *God's Apprentice* ed. E. M. Jackson (London: Hodder & Stoughton, 1991). Since then an illuminating study of Neill's early years (1900-1945) has been published by Dyron Daughrity, *Bishop Stephen Neill: from Edinburgh to South India* (New York: Peter Lang, 2008).

his early teens. It was during one Holy Week, when he himself was convalescing. He describes how, as he reflected on the truth of the atonement, he went to bed one day unconverted but the next day came into an overwhelming sense of God present in his life through Christ. Although brought up in a devoutly evangelical home, it was this conversion experience that he looked as the beginning of his conscious Christian life, the deep knowledge that he was 'in Christ'. He expressed himself as sorry for the 'once born'.[278] As he reflected on the profundity of an experience too easily, in his view, dismissed as an adolescent phenomenon by the unknowing, he wrote in his fiftieth year: 'for those who can look back on some recognisable experience of conversion in their own lives, this is so much more important than anything else that they find it very difficult to take seriously any type of Christian living from which this experience is eliminated'.[279] Nevertheless, he was the first to admit that aspects of the 'old man' remained. He deplored his own 'fierce temper', which continued to plague him after conversion: a rootless childhood and an inability to share what he was learning may have contributed to the problem in so gifted a child. His understanding of Christ as the Truth of God, what some call 'the absoluteness of Christian faith', although he himself was wary of the phrase, of Christ's uniqueness and universal significance, lay in this discovery of Christ in conversion. However open he might be to the treasures hidden in alternative religious traditions, the truth lay for him, as for St. Paul, in that overwhelming experience of God in Christ, the reality of which never left him.

---

[278] Autobiographical MS pp. 60-61. I must express my gratitude here to the Revd. Charles Neill, as literary executor to his uncle, for allowing Christopher Lamb and myself access to this MS towards our two articles. For the position over this MS: see Daughrity, *op cit.*, p. 10 note 34, pp.19-20 and note 79, 80, 81.

[279] S. C. Neill 'Conversion' in *SJT* vol. 3, no. 4 (Dec. 1950), p. 352. This article appeared fifty years to the month after his birth. The writer of this article would add his testimony to Neill's assessment of conversion, as he writes it in the fortieth year since his own. Cf. *God's Apprentice*, pp. 35-6.

Although he might have modified the way in which he expressed himself in later works, he expressed this sense of the finality of Christ in his little book, *The Christian's God* (1954), the first in a series for World Christian Books aimed to educate Christians of the younger churches of which he was general editor: 'since Christ is the "the Truth" we shall not expect to find in those other religions truth which we do not already know. But to look at those other religions will help us to raise important questions in our minds as also to widen our sympathies'.[280] This insistence on Christ as the Truth of God runs like a silver thread through all his theological and missiological enterprise. In another of these small books *What is Man?* (1960) he tried to express something of the mystery of conversion and its relation to baptism in the New Testament. 'If there is a real death, what is it that has died? It is myself. It is that self, which, in its pride, has organised itself in independence of God and in rebellion against Him. And does it want to die? It clings to life with the fury of despair. It is prepared to go to any lengths, to make any kind of compromise with God, if only it can be let off dying. That is why it is so hard to be converted; that is why we must never lightly use the expression: "faith in Jesus Christ". It is always literally a matter of life and death'.[281] One is reminded of Bonhoeffer's words that when Christ calls a man he calls him to come and die. Yet Neill was aware that the 'dying' went on long after conversion: 'this paradox of complete discontinuity, and yet of real continuity of being, is familiar in any experience of conversion. I have the immense advantage of having been definitely converted and therefore can speak from inner experience of this mystery. I have not the smallest doubt that through conversion I became a new man in Christ and that it was literally true that all things became new through Him. And yet I remained distressingly myself. The completely ungovernable temper which was the nightmare of my boyhood remained, though now in an entirely different way under control, as part of my make-up, as a recurring problem or as something that has to be watched over even now… The old man

---

[280]*The Christian's God*, (London: Lutterworth Press, 1954) pp.20-21. The author unless otherwise specified is Neill.
[281]*What is Man?*, (London: Lutterworth Press, 1960) p. 41.

has become new and yet it is the old which has become new and not something else which has taken the place of the old'.[282] With this understanding of conversion as a *metanoia*, which was 'revolutionary, indeed catastrophic'[283] with its sense of discontinuity with all that went before, went this due recognition of the continuity of human life. These insights, which are present in his analysis of conversion, are of considerable importance if we are to understand his view of Christ's entry into history or Christ's advent into another religious tradition, where, as we shall see, Neill saw him as both destroyer and fulfiller. The sense of the catastrophic, the revolutionary, the new which Christ brings, not least through the resurrection, is central: and yet with this is the recognition that this happens in the continuity of human life which we call history or tradition. The integration of these two in a single vision is of great importance to the understanding of Stephen Neill.

The insistence on the importance of conversion was a reiterated theme throughout his life. As a young man, he addressed Anglican evangelicals assembled at Cheltenham on the subject in 1922. The editor of *The Churchman* wrote: 'Nothing could have been finer than the address of Mr Stephen Neill (Trinity College, Cambridge)... Mr Neill deeply moved the conference by his frank description of the theological apathy he finds among his contemporaries, which he attributes to... the (1914-18) war. He is convinced that immediate experience of Christ as our Saviour through belief in the Atonement is the greatest need of our age. Modern preachers do not preach with conviction and are disturbed by all kinds of ideas as to what criticism has discovered. Only one who has been redeemed by Christ and sanctified by his Holy Spirit can manifest the sainthood that must be shown to a world in search of reality'.[284] Later, in his days in India as warden of a theological college in Tinnevelly in 1934 he set himself to solve the difficult problem of the relation of conversion to baptism: 'conversion is essentially self-giving: it is centred in God... the possibility of

---

[282]Review Article 'The Problem of Communication' *SJT*, vol. 1, no. 1 (June 1948) p.45.
[283]'Conversion' *Expository Times* vol. 89, no. 7 (April 1978) p. 205.
[284]*The Churchman* vol. 36, no. 1, NS (July 1922) pp. 224-225.

instantaneous conversion, that the worst sinner who turns to God through faith in Christ does at that moment receive pardon for all his sins and new life … is more than the sacramental regeneration of baptism, in that it is the conscious acceptance of the will of God and therefore makes actual, though not necessarily consciously experienced, the supernatural operation of the Holy Ghost'.[285] In addition to the article already quoted from the *Scottish Journal of Theology* in 1950, with its profound analysis of conversion as primarily affecting the will but with due place for the emotions, he wrote again in the *Expository Times* on the same subject in 1978, complaining that 'in some Christian circles the word "conversion" seems to be regarded almost as a dirty word'.[286] William James' *Varieties of Religious Experience* was in some respects misleading. A new William James was needed, not least to analyse the conversions of those who had been adherents of other faiths: 'here it must be stressed that such conversions are of interest chiefly when the convert has been a strongly convinced adherent of the other faith and yields only with reluctance and even agony to what he has come to be convinced are the higher claims of Jesus Christ. James of course knew something of American missionary work abroad but … a great deal of evidence now before us was simply not available seventy-five years ago'. A start had been made by M. Jarrett-Kerr's *Patterns of Christian Acceptance* (1972) but 'an immense work of sifting, sorting and classification remains to be done. As converts have been won from every known form of religion and every level of culture, if the work is well done the results are likely to be most illuminating'.[287]

Nothing would have delighted Bishop Neill more than that this gap in modern research should catch the eye of some scholar who would devote himself to this subject. It was a need to which he returned frequently towards the end of his life: 'what is it that the contemporary convert has found in Jesus Christ' he wrote in 1984 'that drives him to face exclusion, obloquy, peril, isolation, entrance into an alien world which he often finds cold and

---

[285]*The Churchman* vol. 48, no. 3(July 1934) p. 181.
[286]Art. Cit., *Expository Times*, p. 205, no. 8.
[287]Ibid., p. 207.

unwelcoming? Why is it that he so rarely speaks of his former religion as a preparation for the gospel and much more often as a hindrance ... from which he has escaped with great joy? Many (converts) would answer precisely that they have found here a *salvation* such as they have not found anywhere else and that therefore they must run to receive it, whatever may be the cost'.[288]

Christ and the approach to other faiths

Stephen Neill's main work on the subject of other faiths was the Moorhouse lectures he delivered in Australia in 1960 and published in *Christian Faith and other Faiths* (1961): the sub-title was 'the Christian dialogue with other religions'. After a second edition in the 1970s, a re-written version of it appeared as *Crises of Belief* (1984). The range of reading and erudition displayed is astonishing and not less so when one investigates the other big books, *The Interpretation of the New Testament* (1964) and *The Church and Christian Union* (1968) where equally wide fields of study, with often little overlap, have been digested and elegantly displayed. Neill advocated the way of dialogue. With his background in the Greek classics, he reminded intending participants in inter-faith dialogue that Plato had shown that the object of Socratic dialogue was that truth should emerge. Such dialogue needed to be rigorous and uncompromising: 'we are to enter into this for us alien world as far as may be to understand it as it is understood by those who live within it, not to score points off them or to criticize, but to go as far with them as it is possible to go – and only then to consider whether there may not be a whole dimension in Christian faith of which the partner in the dialogue is unaware but to which perhaps he may be introduced ... nor is there any guarantee that it will lead to the conversion of the other party'. Enrichment will follow as the participant had to rethink his own faith, use terms familiar to others and be faithful to his own body of truth.[289]

---

[288]M. Green (ed.), *The Truth of God Incarnate* (London: Hodder & Stoughton, 1977) p. 86 and Bishop Neill in conversation to the writer.
[289]*The Church and Christian Union* (Oxford: OUP, 1968) pp. 182-3. Cf. *Concise Dictionary of World Missions* (London: Lutterworth Press, 1970) hereafter cited as *Concise* art. 'Dialogue' pp. 165-166.

Like Hendrik Kraemer, Neill was aware that all religions, as all individual lives, are totalities: 'every religion exists as a totality: any particular article of faith is influenced by every other article … Consequently, in any attempt at fusion, each of the bodies which is brought into the alleged unity is bound to suffer a radical transformation and to become something very different from what it was before'.[290] It is a point which Lesslie Newbigin has illustrated well in *The Open Secret* by showing that Peter, as well as Cornelius, was changed by their encounter in Acts 10.[291] What happens however when Christ himself confronts another religious system? Here the position is similar to that experienced in conversion, when he confronts the totality of an individual's life. For every individual brings to conversion his inheritance and culture, family tradition and formation, an inheritance to which Christ is both Judge and Fulfiller. For some of this inheritance Christ means death, for some a new resurrection life. In applying this principle to the inheritance of Judaism, Neill gave a highly stimulating and, to my knowledge, originally expressed contribution to the debate about continuity and discontinuity: it is quoted here with no apology for its length: 'we believe in Christ as the fulfiller of all things. But (we must) … raise the question whether he must not first come as the destroyer before he can be the fulfiller, whether the only way in which he can fulfil human aspirations is first to reduce them to ashes? … Moses and Elijah have died. And yet Moses and Elijah are still alive for us, they are a continuing part of the inheritance that has come to us through patriarchs, prophets, apostles, martyrs. But this is so only because we can now look back at them christologically, we see them as part of that historical preparation which found its culmination in the Christ. It is in his light that they are enlightened; they have died to their own proper being; they are alive for us only because they have risen in the resurrection of the Christ … should we perhaps proceed (to the 'Nay' first). We have recognised this in our own personal experience of passing from death to life. The judgement of Christ has been passed on anything that we were before we knew him: and yet the identity and continuity of our personal life

---

[290]*The Church and the Christian Union*, pp. 171-2.
[291]J. E. L. Newbigin, *The Open Secret* (London: SPCK, 1995) pp. 65-67.

has been maintained. Every religious system is as much an articulated unity as an individual human life. Each one, in its autonomy, in its own self-realisation, is so far in rebellion against God and so far under judgement. But this need not be the last word. As in the case of Judaism, we can learn to read these other religions christologically, to look upon them from the vantage point of the gospel'.[292]

It is to be expected from what has been written to date that Neill would have no truck with an Arnold Toynbee and his suggestion that the Judaeo-Christian tradition should purge itself of exclusive-mindedness and the claim to be unique as a 'sinful state of mind': 'this is surely a very odd piece of argumentation. If Christianity is purged of something that is intrinsic to itself, it will be transformed into something wholly other than itself ... what underlies Professor Toynbee's argument appears to be a curious inability to distinguish between two quite different things, the human arrogance and intolerance which are unable to conceive the possibility that they may themselves be wrong and the awful and necessary intolerance of truth itself'.[293] Neill showed himself sensitive to the prevailing relativism of the pluralist world of the 1980s and continued to set against it the 'awful and necessary intolerance of truth itself'. Although it was attractive, it was inadequate for Will Herberg in *Protestant, Catholic and Jew* to call for the end of talk of conversion as a stage of aggression in religion now past,[294] nor could Neill agree with Reinhold Nebuhr that the Jew should be left in his own traditions 'to find God more easily in terms of his own religious heritage'. If we do this 'have we not yielded to the relativism which is so popular today? The Christian is a Christian because he believes that to have encountered God in Jesus Christ as the word of God is an experience entirely different from any other kind of experience. This being so he cannot do otherwise than desire, not to impose his conviction on others, but to share with all men, Jew and Gentile alike, the unique experience which

---

[292]*Creative Tension* (London: Edinburgh House Press, 1959) pp. 28-29.
[293]Ibid., pp. 11-12
[294]*The Church and the Christian Union*, p. 170.

is his life'.[295] Neill showed his sympathy with the Christian Jew who had said to him that to deny the Jew the opportunity to respond to Christ was an act of anti-Semitism.[296]

With his Jewish friends, 'however humbly', in the cause of theological truth the Christian is bound to raise the question that 'Jesus either is the Messiah of the Jews or he is not'.[297] With the Hindu, tempted to accept Christ as another figure in a syncretist pantheon, the Christian could not neglect that conversion involves joining a community: 'if Christianity meant simply the adoption of good and new ideas about God and man this (remaining within Hinduism) would be a simple and acceptable solution ... but this falls very far short of what the Christian understands by 'conversion' ... (which) involves commitment to a particular Person. On this follows self-dedication to a particular manner of life, in which every detail must be organised in relation to the central loyalty. Such a life can be lived fully only within a community of which every member is ideally inspired by equal loyalty to the divine Head. Thus we come to appreciate that the church ... is not an appendage to the Gospel but an integral part of it'.[298] He recalled Gandhi's friend, C. F. Andrews, who, despite Gandhi's disapproval of the Christian appeal for conversions and despite his deep respect for Gandhi, had stated that 'conversion is necessarily present in any religion which claims to be the truth'.[299] Pluralism cannot be allowed to exclude altogether the question of truth.[300]

---

[295]*Crises of Belief* (London: Hodder and Stoughton, 1984) pp. 42-44.
[296]Ibid., p. 42 note 2.
[297]Ibid., p. 42.
[298]*Crises of Belief*, p. 121.
[299]Green, op. cit., p. 84. Notice here Neill's insistence on the Church and ecclesiology as of prime importance in Christian mission: 'the problem of mission cannot be discussed *inabstracto*; it becomes intelligible only as the mission of the Church. Given a satisfactory ecclesiology ... the answer to all the main problems arising out of Christian mission should be ready to hand. Where no clear doctrine of the Church is held it is not surprising that the missionary problems present themselves as insoluble', *Church and Christian Union*. p. 319.
[300]Ibid., p. 170.

Christ and History

Lesslie Newbigin had judged that Stephen Neill was at heart a historian. He saw himself as primarily a New Testament scholar.[301]The two are not mutually exclusive, for Neill himself emphasised his own background in the study of ancient history and his approval of those, like F. C. Baur, who made the New Testament part of church history. He wrote: 'it was part of my good fortune to be trained in the austere atmosphere of the Cambridge school of ancient history'[302] and he passed severe stricture on those New Testament scholars, of whom he regarded Bornkamm to be one, who came to New Testament studies without training in historical method.[303] His own historical writings were massive achievements: *Anglicanism* (1958) ('of all my books the easiest one to write'[304]), *A History of Christian Missions* (1964), *A History of Christianity in India* (1984-1985). Here we concentrate on his view of history and its importance in theology. For the Christ who has confronted him in conversion, the Christ with whom the alternative religious traditions had to deal as the truth, who acted as both destroyer and fulfiller, was also the Christ who had broken into the continuum of human life with revolutionary and catastrophic effects in the totality of history, and God's new creation.

'He who says "Jesus" says also history'[305] Neill wrote in one of his last essays and he added: 'when Paul uses the simple Jewish name "Jesus" as he does five times in 2 Cor. 4:7-15 he is consciously turning back precisely to that earthly life and to the historical events from which the Christian faith cannot be separated'.[306] In his role as New Testament scholar and notably in his Firth lectures

---

[301]Bishop Newbigin privately to writer. For Neill's self-assessment see the video tapes entitled 'How I changed my mind in mission' in the possession of Dr. G. H. Anderson, Overseas Ministries Centre, New Haven, Connecticut.
[302]Green, op. cit., p. 76.
[303]*The Interpretation of the New Testament 1861-1961*(Oxford: OUP, 1964) p. 279 (hereafter *Interpretation*).
[304]Autobiography MS, p. 594, (or MS 11, p. 24).
[305]Green, op. cit., p. 71.
[306]*Idem.*

The Interpretation of the New Testament 1861-1961 (1964), Neill grappled with the radical historical scepticism of Bultmann and others in relation to the historical Jesus, who, he wrote, 'would reduce Jesus of Nazareth, in the brilliant phrase of the Italian scholar Giovanni Miegge, to the mathematical point which has position but no magnitude'.[307] The fact that we are dependent upon the 'recollections of those who had known him' does not mean that Jesus 'is entirely lost in the mists of history. We may not be able to see him quite as clearly as we should like. But to see him, as we must, through the eyes of others does not mean that we cannot see him at all'.[308] Historians had to be pressed for an account which 'saved the phenomena' and so accounted adequately for the stream of history which flowed from the advent of Jesus. While it is 'certain that a great deal in Jesus Christ will always remain mysterious to us; it is equally certain that the figure which stands behind the Christian movement is greater than either Hitler or Napoleon. That is the way in which history happens; and it can happen in no other way'.[309] It was the fault of a F. C. Baur that he did not allow sufficiently for the *personal* element in history. Once again relativism is the danger. 'If history is no more than the self-realisation of the idea according to the laws of an immanent necessity ... the Christian faith ceases to have anything more than relative significance'.[310] The unique intervention calls for a unique response. But for Neill this uniqueness was historical and empirical.[311] Where Troeltsch was reported to have said, in 1896, that the whole world was tottering on account of the appeal to the

---

[307]*The Supremacy of Jesus* (London: Hodder and Stoughton, 1984) p. 14.
[308]Ibid., p. 15.
[309]*Interpretation*, p.19.
[310]Ibid., p. 28.
[311]Neill never tired of emphasising the 'unique and unrepeatable' nature of history (cf. *Christian Faith and Other Faiths,* 1st edn., (Oxford: OUP, 1961) pp. 8, 17; *Christian Faith Today* (London: Harmondsworth, Penguin, 1955) pp. 18-19; Green op. cit., pp. 72-73). He also pointed to the openness of the historian, as against the philosopher, to the unique and unexpected: 'it is time we learned to think historically: the historian, unlike the philosopher, is prepared to believe in the exceptional', *Expository Times*, vol. 76, no. 1, p. 25.

historical in biblical research, Neill's attitude was very different: 'the historian will throw up his cap to the ceiling with joy at being liberated from the pseudo-certainties of metaphysics and of dogmatic theology into the freedom of his own realm of empiricism and probability'.[312]

The historicity of the resurrection is central to Jesus' uniqueness. Neill took issue with Karl Barth over Barth's dismissal of 1 Cor. 15 as a cardinal piece of documentary evidence for the resurrection. In general, Neill believed that Barth and others had leaned too heavily towards a non-historical Christ.[313] Like Max Warren, he was suspicious of the divorce between salvation history (*Heilgeschichte*) and other history (*Historie*) in the continental theologians. He pointed to St Luke, for whom both strands are the 'same history; each from a different point of view is the story of God's providential government of the nations, all of which he holds in the hollow of his hand.'[314] He asked pertinently of this distinction between 'significant' and 'insignificant' history, as expounded by Bultmann: 'can anything become historically significant if it did not first actually happen?'[315] Further, in Neill's view, Bultmann radically misunderstood the nature of the gospel of the resurrection. For, in the preaching of risen Christ, the hearer is 'not just (confronting) a new understanding of ourselves' in 'what is essentially an old universe' but 'a universe which through the resurrection of Jesus Christ has become wholly new'.[316] History since Pentecost is 'the scene of the new mighty acts of God in history ... the forward march of God among the nations ... (who) gathers out from all the nations a people acceptable to himself'.[317] This in turn meant that the missionary movement of the church, which he viewed correctly as grossly underestimated by professional academic historians, was in fact 'the great creative

---

[312]Green, op. cit., p. 74.
[313]*Interpretation*, p. 209, note 2.
[314]Ibid., pp. 267-268.
[315]Ibid., pp. 233-235.
[316]'Theology 1939-64', *Expository Times*, vol. 76, no. 1, (Oct. 1964), p. 25.
[317]*Interpretation*, p. 268.

force in human history'.[318] The missionary has an importance and significance which has again been gravely underestimated[319] for there is a real sense that it is not until the gospel is preached in a particular nation or culture that history in the strict sense begins: 'the missionary is engaged the whole time in making history, divine history'.[320] As with an individual life, up to the advent of Christ there is a natural succession of events: but for Neill as for Paul, when Christ enters in 'all things become new', there is a new creation (2 Cor. 5:21) and something 'catastrophic and revolutionary' has entered in so that nothing can be the same again. 'Theologically history is important. If we believe that in Jesus Christ God did finally and definitively intervene in the world of men, we are committed to the view that history is the chosen sphere of his working and that therefore history, all history, including history of you and me today, is related to the process of revelation'.[321] History at large and our personal history have become significant when they interact with the activity of God in Christ.

Neill realised both the importance and the limitations of history in relation to Christian faith. He was well aware that to say all this 'is not for a moment to suggest that the certainties of faith can be made to rest on the contingencies of history'.[322] Greater information about Jesus would not establish a 'single grain of faith'. But the converse idea was not true: historical research cannot establish faith but in certain circumstances it could destroy it, if it could be established, for example, that Jesus never existed at all.[323] Again, Neill was well aware of the tension, expressed classically by Troeltsch, between the demands of detachment and

---

[318]*The Church and Christian Union*, p.94.
[319]*Interpretation*, p.268.
[320]Ibid., p. 268-275.
[321]Ibid., p. 290
[322]*The Church and Christian Union*, p. 130. Cf. Neill on Lessing's comment that the 'contingent truths of history cannot serve as proof for the unchanging truths of the intellect' in *Crises of Belief*, pp. 113-114. Christian thinkers have been 'bewitched' into viewing Christianity as a religion of ideas by this dictum.
[323]*The Church and Christian Union*, p. 130.

objectivity and the commitment of faith held simultaneously in the same person. Again he quoted Miegge with approval on this issue: 'by standing firm in this tension; by bringing day to day the results of our labours as historians into confrontation with the institutions of our faith; without allowing these historical results, from which the element of the transcendent is systematically excluded, to blot out for us the vision of that world of certainties and of higher values which is the concern of faith and from which alone history can derive its significance and values; and without on the one hand allowing this higher significance, as a too facile explanation, surreptitiously to take the place of the labour of historical research. This attitude is no more than the adaptation to the terms of our daily work of our faith in Christ, which is truly that the incarnation is the ruling principle from which the Christian understanding of history is derived'.[324] Certainly, 'historical Christology' and 'Christological history' were marks of Stephen Neill's work as theologian and historian; and it was an important part of his remarkable achievement to integrate the two in his own vision, while, in his historical work, retaining a high degree of objectivity and detachment, which the necessary compression of this article has been in danger of under-emphasising.

Conclusion

Although Stephen Neill never formally brought these strands of his thought into a synthesis it may be legitimate to attempt a general interpretation at this point. Every life, every religion, even history itself can be viewed as a totality. Into this totality Christ has appeared, bringing with him God's new creation. Neill himself, in his conversion, had experienced that rebirth, the element of the wholly new which breaks into the continuum of natural life with the in-coming of Christ by the Holy Spirit. The old, however, remains. In his coming and his continuing presence, Christ acts as destroyer and fulfiller, passing judgement in individual lives and in

---

[324]G. Miegge, *Visible and Invisible*, tr. by S. C. Neill, pp. 100-101 and quoted in *The Church and Christian Union*, pp. 98-99. For Troeltsch accessibly expressed see the essay 'The Place of Christianity among the World Religions' in J. Hick and B. Hebblethwaithe, *Christianity and other Religions* (London: Collins, Fount, 1980) pp. 11-31.

the great world of religious traditions, on all that cannot bear the light because, in Johannine language, the 'deeds are evil': but equally, with the inherited traditions that the individual brings with him to conversion, whether for Christians or for those from non-Christian cultures. Christ acts as fulfiller of all that is good and true. The base is judged and destroyed: the lovely and that of good report finds in him fulfilment. In regard to history, for Neill there is a real renewal of the whole order by God's action in Christ, a break in continuity, radical, revolutionary, 'catastrophic'. The old persists but it is viewed by us, like Moses and Elijah, from the vantage point of the new order. This in turn sets new priorities for the historian and gives a new importance to the spread of the gospel of new life among the nations. It gives great significance to the missionary, as the bearer of the seed of a new and significant history, linked to the purposive and redemptive activity of God. One cannot believe that someone with so high a view of the Greek classics thereby intended them for a historical limbo: but they too, the Aeschylus, Sophocles, Plato and Aristotle of his quotations are subject to the same radically renewed vision since Christ and the resurrection; and their significance, so real to Neill himself, comes from those aspects of the truth which they contain which is risen in Christ.

Like St. Paul, Stephen Neill found the truth of God through conversion to Christ. Like Paul, he devoted his intellectual life to 'bringing every thought into captivity to Christ' (2 Cor. 10:5). This involved him in immense erudition in various fields of intellectual activity. It also involved, as the autobiography indicates, great turmoil, very great physical and psychological difficulties which led him at times to the brink of suicide via insomnia and depression, the kind of personal cost known often to the superbly gifted and creative but outside the ken of many more ordinary mortals.[325] He has left us overwhelmingly in his debt. The whole of his amazing *corpus* of study and writing was directed to the cause of truth and this truth he expected to exalt the Christ whom he had discovered in young life to be the Truth. Any short article must be

---

[325]Autobiographical MS, pp. 85-98; *God's Apprentice*, pp. 7, 9, 115. This paper was published in *Anvil*, Vol. 5, No. 2, pp. 151-61.

wholly inadequate to convey the wealth of his theological legacy, let alone the elegance and lucidity and lightness of touch with which it is conveyed. This will have done its part if it encourages a new generation of Christian thinkers, not least among evangelical Anglicans, to enter into the riches of the inheritance bequeathed to us.

CHAPTER 8
by Stephen Skuce

DT NILES: THE LAST OF THE GREAT METHODISTS

In the aftermath of World War II, when the wisdom of a generation of leaders had led much of the world to global conflict, the ecumenical movement, seeking to escape from this history turned to a relatively young Asian to preach at the opening worship and help initiate the first assembly of the WCC. The somewhat precocious Niles was an excellent choice and this pivotal role points to the significance of this Ceylonese Methodist minister.

I never personally met DT Niles but I do have a somewhat obscure link. For two years I was minister of Maradana Methodist Church in Colombo, an appointment held by Niles forty five years previously. Given the fairly rapid change of Methodist ministers in such appointments in Sri Lanka, the local church authorities often do not keep advising the various utility providers of the new minister's name. So, as regards the good people of Sri Lanka Telecom, I was DT Niles. Every couple of months the bill would arrive in Niles' name, and I would duly pay it. Sri Lanka Telecom considered I was good enough to stand in for Niles, and that was enough for me.

After a very brief biographical portrait I offer some assessment of the contribution of Niles in his era, and what his enduring contribution is for us today. Niles lived in a generation when Methodists gave a very significant lead in ecumenism and mission thinking. While still significant in ecumenical thinking, the Methodist contribution to missiology has trailed away. It is important for Methodists and Wesleyans today to understand the contribution of Niles in the past, that it might challenge our present and help determine our future.

The Life of DT Niles (1908-1970)

Daniel Thambyrajah Niles, always known as DT, was born in Jaffna, the historic northern centre of Tamil learning and culture in the then Ceylon.[326] His family were historically Christian for the previous 100 years and contained a number of Methodist ministers. The son of a judge, Niles studied at Union Theological College, Bangalore, India, and later graduated with a doctorate from the University of London. Married to Dulcie with sons Preman and Dayalan, Niles served as a Ceylonese Methodist minister in local appointments and on a world stage.

Niles' appointments and the significant events he contributed to read like a history of both the ecumenical and mission movements in the mid twentieth century. This list on its own is impressive but I have included this as Niles was remarkable in being prominent at national, regional and international levels while maintaining an ongoing local ministry throughout. When you consider that for much of this time he lived in Ceylon without electricity or a personal phone line, the range of involvement is truly remarkable.

Within Methodism

Ordained as Methodist minister	1936
District Evangelist of Methodist Church	
Ceylon North District	1936-39
Minister, Methodist Church Point Pedro	1946-50
Minister, Methodist Church Maradana	1950-53
Principal Jaffna Central College	1953-62
Chairman of Methodist Church Ceylon North District	1954-64
Superintendent Minister, Jaffna	1953-59
Member World Methodist Council	1961-70
President of Ceylon Methodist Conference	1968-70

Within World Christianity

National Secretary,	
Ceylon Student Christian Movement	1933-36
Speaker at IMC Tambaram	1938

---

[326] I will use Ceylon as the normal national name. Ceylon became Sri Lanka in 1972, not long after Niles' death.

Director of Evangelism, World YMCA (Geneva)	1939-40
General Secretary National Council of Churches, Ceylon	
	1941-45
Preacher at opening service of WCC Assembly	
(Amsterdam)	1948
Chair of Youth Dept, WCC	1948-52
Executive Secretary Evangelism Dept, WCC	1953-59
Chair, World Student Christian Federation	1953-60
Speaker at WCC Assembly (Evanston)	1954
Visiting Professor, Union Theological Seminary,	
New York	1959-60
General Secretary, East Asia Conference of Churches	1957-68
Speaker at WCC Assembly (New Delhi)	1961
President, East Asia Conference of Churches	1968-70
Opening preacher at WCC Assembly (Uppsala)	1968
President, WCC	1968-70

The Contribution of DT Niles
Wesleyan Theologian

Niles has not always been recognised as a theologian. Indeed, he was self-deprecating when reflecting that he did not claim 'either adequate scholarship or accuracy of method'.[327] What he did do, either deliberately or instinctively as a Wesleyan, was to integrate Scripture with tradition and experience to produce work that was reasonable and consequently spoke to his generation.

Systematic theology was not his interest,[328] and Niles managed to avoid significant comment on any major doctrinal discussions of his era. It was the outworking of doctrine in how it impacted the lives of those around him that was Niles' focus; experimental rather than systematic or dogmatic theology, a Wesleyan characteristic. His writings covered mission, ecumenism, Bible study and the application of faith to the world. Influences included

---

[327] Niles, DT, *Studies in Genesis* (Philadelphia; Westminster Press, 1958), p. 18.
[328] Niles ,WD 'Search for Community: A preliminary Explanation of the Theology of DT Niles' Paper delivered at the Oxford Institute for Methodist Theological Studies, Oxford, 1977, p.8.

E Stanley Jones who stressed the immanence of God, Hendrik Kraemer who helped Niles understand his Christian faith in relation to other faiths, and PD Devanandan who enabled Niles to appreciate how those of other faiths might view Christianity.[329] Niles' final book started as a systematic presentation of the Christian message but 'once begun, it took the form simply of a personal testament of faith.'[330] The Wesleyan stress on testimony as response to God rather than a dogmatic articulation won the day.

Rather than coming from a narrow doctrinaire position, Niles exampled the generous orthodoxy of the Wesleyan view where he held on to the objective truths of the Christian faith but was able to engage with others. Faith was to be shared and discovered rather than defended. Niles' orthodoxy can be seen in *We Know in Part* where he argued that the rationalism and scepticism of Bishop Robinson's *Honest to God* lacked a full understanding of humanity's response to God. No matter how important it was to present the Christian message in language that spoke to a contemporary world, this could not be at the loss of orthodoxy.

In good Wesleyan tradition Niles was a hymn writer. This was not his major contribution and he is not the Asian Charles Wesley. But, he fully recognised that theology was not a static body of propositions to which people might assent, but rather in Wesleyan understanding theology was to be expressed in a variety of ways and was part of people's response to God. A practical theologian, Niles sought to communicate Christian truth and hymns were one very appropriate medium for this. Theology was sung and celebrated more than taught.[331]

---

[329] Lacy, C, 'The Legacy of DT Niles', *International Bulletin of Missionary Research,* (Oct, 1984), p. 175.
[330] Niles , DT, *A Testament of Faith* (London: Epworth, 1972), p.7.
[331] Niles had three hymns in the British Methodist hymnal *Hymns and Psalms* (Peterborough: Methodist Publishing House, 1983) and one in the successor hymnal *Singing the Faith* (London: Methodist Publishing House, 2011)

Perhaps more notable as a preacher, a number of Niles' published works were collections of sermons.[332]   Again he follows a Wesleyan practice of expounding scripture rather than writing abstract theology and so the Christian faith is 'in its essence, an event to be declared'.[333] In artwork John Wesley is normally shown preaching from the Bible rather than studying the Bible. Clearly Bible study occurred, but it was study so that the fruits could be shared dynamically. This was also the way of DT Niles. Many of the chapters of his books followed a common pattern. A subject would be tackled from Scripture, the writing of others including the hymns of Charles Wesley would be engaged with, and an outcome that made sense of current reality was produced. He wrote as he preached. Niles most systematic work, *Upon the Earth*, written on behalf of the WCC, is a good example of this preaching style.[334]   One quirk to this style was the regular quoting of Charles Wesley's hymns but very sparse reference to the writings of John Wesley.

Inter-faith understanding, a lived reality in Sri Lanka, was important to Niles and he was one of a number who introduced and promoted the importance of dialogue into world Christianity before it was commonplace. At least a decade ahead of most, in the 1950s Niles was arguing for the need to present the gospel to all whilst recognising that those who are not Christian may still be living within the orbit of Christ's saving work.[335] But it would be wrong to take any inclusiveness too far. In commenting on the faiths found in Sri Lanka Niles argued 'Buddhism, Islam,

---

332 See Niles, DT, *Preaching the Gospel of the Resurrection* (London: Lutterworth, 1953); *The Preacher's Task and the Stone of Stumbling* (New York: Harper & Brothers, 1958); *The Preacher's Calling to be Servant* (New York: Harper & Brothers, 1959) and *Whereof we are Witnesses* (London: Epworth, 1965)

333 Niles, DT, *Whereof we are Witnesses* (London: Epworth, 1965), p. 17.

334 Niles, DT *Upon the Earth: The Mission of God and the Missionary Enterprise of the Church* (London: Lutterworth, 1962). In chapter 1 Niles quotes from three of Charles Wesley's hymns.

335 Lacy, C, 'The Legacy of DT Niles', *International Bulletin of Missionary Research,* (Oct, 1984), p. 176.

Hinduism – they represent the settled ways of our people. They are the "past" which an infant Church confronts, as it seeks to make Christ known, loved and obeyed.'[336] In *The Preacher's* Task Niles deals with Hindu, Muslim and Buddhist theological rejections of the Christian message, and some more personal obstacles to followers of those faiths turning to Christ. Charles Wesley's hymns are again quoted with gusto, and there is no doubt that the Christian task 'is to make disciples for Jesus Christ among all the nations.[337] Niles had a knack of pointing to the supremacy of Christ without denigrating the faith of another. In *Reading the Bible Today* he recounts a personal illustration where he prayed for a Hindu friend whose wife was dying and reflects 'Indeed, there is no one else to go to.'[338] Like John Wesley, Niles had a generous understanding about the possibility of God at work in the life of someone of another faith, but Christ was still to be presented to all.

Young and Asian

At Amsterdam in 1948 Niles' youth and nationality allowed Niles to represent the future with perhaps the past being demonstrated in the elderly John Mott, as they both preached at the opening of the first assembly. His Ceylonese nationality placed him in what was to become the developing or majority world, but Niles' British colonial heritage and education and, vitally, an excellent command of English made him accessible to the historic world. He exampled the change that was both desired, and was starting to be experienced, although he was certainly a forerunner to the later developments that more fully recognised the global dimension to the Christian faith, and the need to escape from the stereotype of white, male, middle-aged English language speakers.

Niles recognised that he was at a turning point in history. The growing independence of the African and Asian countries would soon be matched by the move away from a western dominated Christianity. Ceylon became independent in the same year as the

---

[336] Niles, DT, *Reading the Bible Today* (London: Lutterworth, 1955), p. 76.
[337] Niles, *The Preacher's Task and the Stone of Stumbling*, p.35.
[338] Niles, *Reading the Bible Today*, p. 71.

first WCC assembly, and perhaps it is no surprise that it was an Asian from a newly independent nation, rather than an African from what would still have been a colony, who represented the future. It would be inaccurate to consider Niles' importance as largely because of what he represented, but reasons why an individual rises to prominence more than some others often contain an element beyond individual control.

Mission

As an evangelist Niles exhibited the holistic gospel that has become widely recognised within the Christian movement today, but was less central in a previous age. A product of the missionary era, Niles was comfortable with presenting the Christian message with the hope that others would turn to Christ. Many of his responsibilities were related to evangelism and he preached evangelistically wherever he was. In an era of Christian institutions, he recognised that such institutions could not in themselves be evangelistic enterprises if their declared purpose was to care for the needs of others.[339]

Famously stating that evangelism was 'one beggar telling another beggar where to get food',[340] Niles was one of a number of figures who recognised that the imperial presentation of the gospel as a package containing western civilisation and colonialism was not effective in Asia and was not true to the gospel itself. His approach of humility reflects that of E Stanley Jones. At times Niles was content not to argue for the truth of the gospel, but simply to present Christ as 'Jesus substantiates His own claim. When He is lifted up, He draws; when He is sown, He grows; when He is presented, He captivates; in His presence, other lights pale.'[341]

---

[339] Niles, *Upon the Earth*, p. 262.
[340] Niles, DT, *That they may have Life* (New York: Harper & Brothers, 1951), p. 96.
[341] Niles, *Whereof we are Witnesses*, p. 15.

Ecumenism

Methodism, for its size, has been over represented in the ecumenical movement if WCC general secretaries are used as a category.[342] Niles was a vital part of the Methodist contribution to the development of the ecumenical world, being involved at national, regional and world level. He straddled the missionary dominant era of the International Missionary Council, and then the post world war creation of the WCC. This involvement in the WCC is well recognised, and his list of contributions as preacher, speaker, office holder and finally as a President stands as testimony to the recognition of Niles by others. Perhaps it is worth noting the youthfulness at which many of these responsibilities were taken up. Niles was no elder statesman given honours; he was an energetic activist given jobs to do to develop world Christianity.

Not given as much attention as it merited was Niles' involvement in the East Asian Christian Council (EACC). He was the driving force in bringing national churches together in an era when their denominational loyalty normally overruled regional alliances. The EACC was to be the pattern of a number of other ecumenical schemes. The EACC *Hymnal*, largely Niles' creation as General Editor, is an important part of the journey to escape from western liturgical formulations as the norm from which others might deviate. Niles helped to establish other norms.

Ironically it was within Ceylon where his ecumenical vision failed to carry the day. A Church Union scheme was mooted as early as 1934, substantive proposals emerged in 1955 but the ambitious scheme, which included Anglicans, Methodists, Presbyterians and Baptists, finally floundered in the mid 1960s.[343] While much of the documentation bears the insights of Niles, it was unsuccessful.

---

[342] Since Niles death WCC general secretaries have included three Methodists, namely Philip Potter, Emilio Castro and Samuel Kobia.
[343] See Negotiating Committee for Church Union in Ceylon *Proposed Scheme of Church Union in Ceylon* (Colombo: The Negotiating Committee, 1964). The Methodist Church of Ceylon narrowly voted against the scheme.

It may be that the force of personality Niles was able to exert in the various ecumenical offices he held was absent in the church union discussions in Ceylon where he had no formal responsibilities. Visser t'Hooft was among many who noted Niles' focus on achieving outcomes, commenting about the EACC that Niles 'came to the meeting with very definite ideas as to the results at which it should arrive. And since he had given more thought to the subject than other participants, he was often able to convince the meeting that his plan should be accepted.'[344] While this was usually true at regional and international level, it was not so within his own denomination's consideration of formal unity.

Methodist Church
Part of Niles' strength was that he remained rooted within the Methodist Church of Ceylon and made an ongoing contribution to that denomination. In addition to his ecumenical contribution, Niles was fully involved throughout his ministry in leadership of local congregations, of Methodist districts, and in the national denomination. Some who have become 'world Christian statesmen' have, through necessity of international responsibilities, travel etc, become somewhat divorced from local responsibilities. Niles managed to combine the local, national and international, and so his contribution was within Ceylon as much as it was to the wider world. He provided an excellent model of a missionary pastor and scholar to his own denomination as well as to others.

The Importance of DT Niles Now
Almost fifty years after his death, Niles is less well remembered than some of his contemporaries. The world has moved on, and a number of areas where Niles was at the cusp have developed so quickly that his contribution is now very historic. However, there are some areas where the benefit of hindsight shows Niles was somewhat prophetic and issues where his insights are still important to consider.

---

344 Visser t'Hooft, WA 'DT Niles' *International Review of Mission* Vol LX No 237 (Jan 1971), p. 119

Mission

Rereading *Upon the Earth* fifty years after its first publication reveals a number of areas where it is apparent that it is an historical text. There is a sense of the author knowing the significance of what was written and that the Christian community was at a pivotal moment. The certainties of Christendom were being left behind and Niles, in company with such dialogue partners as Mott, Newbigin, Jones, Kraemer and Devanandan was pointing to the future.

Parts of this work have dated. There is a focus on communism that seems quaint today and the use of gender exclusive language jars. Niles' discussion of 'older' and 'younger' churches is happily consigned to history. However, he recognised before most a number of the challenges and opportunities that were to impact the Church. So, he points to the growth of Pentecostalism although in 1962 it was hard for others to imagine that the twentieth century would become known as a Pentecostal century for Christian historians.[345] Niles recognised the need for the Church to be generous in its social understanding in relationship to polygamy.[346] A challenge facing the Church today is seeking to fully understand gender and sexual identity issues.

When Niles wrote of the need for the western Church to win the general population of their nations for Christ he was recognising the decline of western Christianity and that the certainties of Christendom could no longer be assumed.[347] Combined with his challenge to the Church to escape from western individualism and rediscover family worship and authentic community, Niles demonstrated then what is more apparent now.[348] Today the weakness of western Christianity is clear, as is the reality that the future of world Christianity is to be found outside the west. This was not widely recognised in 1962 but Niles pointed both to the reality of western Christian decline, but more crucially that

---

[345] Niles, *Upon the Earth,* p.211.
[346] Niles, *Upon the Earth*, p.203.
[347] Niles, *Upon the Earth,* p.202.
[348] Niles, *Upon the Earth,* p.108.

western Christianity was not in itself the zenith of Christian expression. It was culturally bound in ways that were unhelpful to Christian mission, and that denied parts of the gospel.

Niles pointed to the crucial role of lay people in renewing the Church, perhaps less obvious in his more clerically focused generation.[349] And he recognised that Christian mission is one and so 'going from New York to Sierra Leone with the gospel cannot be theologically different from taking the Gospel within New York to East Harlem'.[350] It was Newbigin among others in the 1980s whose constant repetition of this message helped the western Church to recognise that the west was now (and always had been) a mission field and so the insights of cross cultural mission practitioners were crucial. As Christianity continues to decline in the west but grow in other regions, openness to the insights of others remains crucial.

While he could not have imagined the impact of globalisation, the internet and social media, Niles had enough insight to challenge the Church as necessarily having a geographical entity by his recognition of the value of networks based on occupation rather than location to help define church.[351] This is a challenge that needs to be more fully addressed.

Young and Asian
While world Christianity has moved on dramatically since Niles' death in 1970, with developments in South America, Korea and Africa perhaps the most dramatic, the dominance of western Christianity is still very strong. English language is still a factor, as is western education and the ability to communicate in ways that others recognise. In Africa the Church has come of age and in many areas is large, vibrant and involved in mission across the world, although more often focused on national diasporas in a way very similar to the era that predated the 19th century western missionary project.

---

349 Niles, *Upon the Earth,* pp.147-8.
350 Niles, *Upon the Earth,* p.260.
351 Niles, *Upon the Earth,* p.259.

But, more than language, it is still finance that dominates. Korea, with an American focus although far from uniform use of English, is a powerhouse of world Christianity but often perpetuates the mistakes of older western Christianity in using finance to control.[352] It is no longer European or even North American mission partners who are met in obscure corners of the world, but more often Koreans who finance and control their ministry without placing it under local authority. As a young Asian, Niles represented a potential future without control from abroad. He was from an independent nation, if not yet an autonomous church, for most of his ministry. This full independence has yet to be fully achieved. It might be without independence there cannot be interdependence.

There is a quirk in that the future of world Christianity may still be young and Asian. The decades since Niles' death have seen the rise of Korean Christianity, but it may well be in China that Christianity finds its future. In Niles' era the expulsion of western missionaries and the communist control of that nation may have meant that China was considered one of the major obstacles to the gospel. Today it may well be the future.

Ecumenism
Niles pointed to a risk that the rise of international confessional bodies, for example the World Lutheran Federation, brought to the ecumenical vision.[353] He rightly recognised that pointing national expressions of denominational Christianity to others of the same denomination elsewhere, rather than other Christians in their immediate geography, could negatively impact ecumenism. It should not be a surprise that the development of national united/uniting Churches has largely ceased as the international confessional bodies continue to grow in significance. However, perhaps the main challenge from this that remains is the need for ecumenism, that the world might believe. The historic and still largely ecumenical denominations have been eclipsed in many parts of the world by new denominations and networks with looser

---

[352] Niles, *Upon the Earth,* p.203.
[353] Niles, *Upon the Earth,* p. 219.

ecclesiology who often understand church planting where there is already a plethora of denominations as appropriate as it widens choice and spurs each other on through competition.

The era of mission comity is a very distant memory but the Christian world needs to rehear Niles' ecumenical challenge. Unless Christians are one the world will not believe. Too often ecumenists are not particularly missional and mission practitioners are not very ecumenical. Niles combined both and brings both a challenge and a personal example for today.

Wesleyan Theologian
As a missiologist Niles recognised that it is the Christian message that engages with other faiths. Following Barth, the Christian Church stands under the same judgement as other religious systems. Niles could not have foretold the various abuse and other scandals that have impacted the Christian Church in the twenty-first century but he rightly recognised that while the Church would not win the world for Christ, that Christ could and would. His confidence was not in the institutional Church but in the message. Few today have the confidence in the institution that some previous generations had, but many have also lost confidence in the message. Within British Methodism, there is a need to recognise the weakness of the institution but the reality of the power of the message. Niles had this, and British Methodism needs this today.

In the years since Niles many Christians have moved from embracing pluralism and thinking that necessitated a rejection of evangelism, to a questioning of pluralism but without an answer. The question remains as to how Christian faith relates to the beliefs of the world? With a generous view of others, Niles had the confidence to answer that 'there is true and essential discontinuity. The Christian message cannot be grafted upon other beliefs or added to them. There is only one way in which the Christian message can be accepted and that is by a radical conversion to it.'[354] He spoke both about the relationship between Christian faith

---

[354] Niles, *Upon the Earth*, p. 243.

and the faith of others, and actively shared Christ with all. The evangelistic dimension is too often lacking in contemporary inter-faith encounter and Niles practice as much as his insight needs to be recaptured.

Methodist Church
Was Niles the last of the great Methodists? That is hard to determine but he was the last of the great Methodist missiological and ecumenical innovators. By the end of Niles' life mission was starting to be understood as one task wherever in the world, and the ecumenical world structures had been created. Other Methodists followed who became general secretaries of the WCC and held influential positions but Niles was the last to impact the breadth of contexts. He influenced local and world Methodism; he influenced local and world Christianity.

In the twentieth century the three great Methodists were John Mott, E Stanley Jones and DT Niles. They were all missiologists and ecumenists. They lived out the Wesleyan understanding of the Catholic Spirit and sought to win all for Christ. Contemporary Methodism has produced ecumenical figures of note, but somewhat lost its way missiologically. The challenge from Niles is to integrate mission with all aspects of the life of the Church. While they have yet to emerge, God willing there will be twenty first century names that can be said alongside that of DT Niles.

CHAPTER 9

READING JOHN V. TAYLOR

John Vernon Taylor (1914-2001) was the son of J.R.S. Taylor, a scholar at Cambridge, where John was born on September 11, 1914. John's father gained a first-class degree in classics, served on the staff at Ridley Hall (1910-17), and eventually became headmaster of St. Lawrence School, Ramsgate, a boys' boarding school on the south coast of England. John later wrote that at the school he remembered meeting Christian visitors from around the world – Indians, Chinese, and Africans – who stimulated his imagination toward future service in the mission field.[355] His father became principal of Wycliffe Hall in Oxford, like Ridley Hall a leading Anglican college for training for the ordained ministry, and John studied there from 1936, when his father was head of the college. The father later became an Anglican bishop, a vocation in which John followed him after curacies at All Souls, Langham Place (1938-40), in London and at St. Helen's Lancashire (1940-43). Between these two curacies John married his lifelong partner Peggy, who had been a student at the Royal School of Music in London. John later was a missionary in Uganda, with spells as both Africa secretary and general secretary of the Church Mission (ary) Society (CMS). In 1975 he became bishop of Winchester.

A recent thesis rightly describes John Taylor as 'priest and prophet...also a poet'.[356] Taylor, who had an artistic temperament, composed poetry (e.g. *A Christmas Sequence and Other Poems* [1989]), produced an African passion play when he was principal of a theological college in Uganda, and directed Jonathan Harvey's religious opera *Passion and Resurrection* in Winchester cathedral as bishop. His chief means of expression, however, were his books

---

355 John V. Taylor, 'My Pilgrimage in Mission,' *IBMR* 17 (April 1993): 59.
356 David G. Wood, 'Bishop John V. Taylor: Poet, Priest, and Prophet: Christian Mission in the Global Village' (Ph. D. thesis, Univ. of Monash, Melbourne, Australia, 2000), p.13.

and writings, such as his CMS newsletters. He was a writer of high calibre, with a wide range of interests, including missionary theology, Christian doctrine, biblical theology, and studies leaning on anthropology and sociology in their analysis of African life and the life of African churches. When in 1963 he became general secretary of CMS, a society founded by Charles Simeon, John Venn, and William Wilberforce, Taylor entered into a long and distinguished inheritance of Anglican evangelical leaders. It included the great nineteenth century secretaries Josiah Pratt (1802-24) and Henry Venn, the younger (1841-72), whose work was recorded memorably by the historian and missionary administrator Eugene Stock in his three-volume *History of the Church Missionary Society* (1899).

In the twentieth century CMS was also served by some remarkable figures. Max Warren, general secretary from 1942 to 1963, had an influence equivalent to that of Henry Venn. In the 1940s Warren was approached by Taylor, then a young Cambridge graduate who had studied English literature and history at Cambridge, as well as theology at Oxford. Taylor told Warren that he believed that he had a call to the mission field but was unsure of it.[357] Warren told him that there was a place for a man with his qualifications in Uganda, as principal of the main training centre for Anglican clergy for the Church of Uganda, at Bishop Tucker College, near Kampala. Taylor accepted the challenge and became one of the most sensitive interpreters of things African to fellow Europeans of the twentieth century. After ten years at Bishop Tucker College (1944-54), he served with the International Missionary Council (IMC) as a research worker in Africa (1954-59), then was based in London as Africa secretary of CMS (1959-63), before succeeding Max Warren as general secretary (1963-75). He continued to write as bishop (1975-85) and, from 1985, in retirement in Oxford.

Taylor's writings fall into three identifiable groups, broadly sequential: (1) his books on Africa; (2) his writings while general secretary of CMS, a period that included his newsletters, which, like Warren's, were and are a considerable theological and

---

[357] Taylor, 'My Pilgrimage,' p. 59.

missiological resource; and (3) his volumes on Christian doctrine, of which the most widely read was probably *The Go-Between God: The Holy Spirit and the Christian Mission* (1972). During his time as bishop of Winchester, Taylor became chairman of the Church of England's Doctrine Commission.

Africa

Other Europeans have been sensitive interpreters of African traditions and religion, among them Edwin Smith, born in Africa of Methodist missionary parents, who gained an international reputation as an anthropologist; Geoffrey Parrinder, author of *African Traditional Religions* (1954); and the Belgian Placide Tempels, author of *La Philosophie Bantoue* (1945). Nevertheless, Taylor's *Primal Vision* was recognised as very important in this field and is so still. In this section, I will concentrate on it among his African works, but not before noting in passing various contrasts, tensions, and dichotomies in the other books also, to which I return in the conclusion of this article.

Taylor's first book, *Christianity and Politics in Africa* (1957), was a plea for Christians to engage with political realities. He showed how ardent Christians – for example, those touched by the East African revival of the 1930s that was still a strong force when he wrote – could view political life as corrupting, besmirching the purity of the soul, staining the Christian believer. He recognised that the urge to create an alternative and purer society had roots in the New Testament, but for Taylor this impulse was not the whole truth. He was able to balance the account of the revival brethren by pointing to two prime ministers of the kingdoms of Uganda who in 1954 were members of the revival brethren.[358] Here was a spiritual-material, spiritual-political tension, something he also found in the followers of the prophetess Alice Lenshina in the Lumpa Church, which he investigated during his research for the

---

358 John V. Taylor, *Christianity and Politics in Africa* (London: Penguin Books, 1957) pp. 18-19.

125

IMC in *Christians in the Copperbelt* (modern Zambia) of 1961. He wrote that this church 'exhibits an emphatic otherworldliness.'[359]

In his other piece of research for the IMC, *The Growth of the Church in Buganda* (1958), a church-growth book before the topic became popular, Taylor noticed the tension between African and European worldviews, a topic to which he returned in the *Primal Vision*. While the African aimed to live in harmony with nature, the European aimed to control and dominate it; while the African was in touch with his or her instincts, the European suffered from 'spiritual sickness of the heart, which reveals itself in the division of the sacred from the secular, of the cerebral from the instinctive,' a breaking of a harmony that 'the wisdom of Africa has not yet thrown away.'[360] In a phrase coined by T.S. Eliot, Africans were among those who could still 'think their feelings and feel their thoughts,' something many Europeans had lost.

The title *The Primal Vision* (1967) suggest clarity of perception on these and other matters that is present in many societies, not just African ones, where there is an integrated view of life and the cosmos – in our terms, a holistic view. This perspective refuses to see people as isolated individuals but, in contrast to Descartes' 'I think, therefore I am,' affirms, 'I participate, therefore I am.'[361] John Mbiti made the same point in saying, 'I am because we are.'[362] Taylor quoted Father Tempels on the Bantu: '[They] cannot conceive a man as an individual existing by himself, unrelated to the animate and the inanimate forces surrounding him. It is not sufficient to say he is a social being; he feels himself a vital force in actual intimate and permanent rapport with the other forces – a vital force both influenced by and influencing them.'[363]

---

359 John V. Taylor and Dorothea A. Lehmann, *Christianity of the Copperbelt* (London: SCM Press, 1961), p. 165.
360 John V. Taylor, *The Growth of the Church in Buganda* (London: SCM Press, 1958), p. 259.
361 John V. Taylor, *The Primal Vision* (London: SCM Press, 1963), p.50.
362 John S. Mbiti, *African Religions and Philosophy* (London: SCM Press, 1963), pp. 108-9.
363 Placide Tempels, *Bantu-filosofie,* p. 30, quoted in Taylor, *Primal Vision*, p. 30.

Taylor wrote: 'A man's well-being consists in keeping in harmony with the cosmic totality.' When that harmony is broken and has to be restored, then divination is called for to discern how restoration may take place.[364]

In an earlier book Taylor had wondered whether the High God had ever really figured in African traditional religion among the Buganda until introduced to Islam.[365] There, as well as in *Primal Vision*, he saw the divinisation of dead kings and heroes as the real link with the unseen world, a feature common in primal societies. In *Primal Vision*, however, Taylor seems to have come to a point where, despite his awareness of the ethnological debate on the issue of the High God, he found it 'impossible to dispute a universal recognition of and desire for the Ultimate God,' shown not least in songs, proverbs, and riddles, which 'reveal the deep sense of a pervading presence' of the God who is met everywhere and who fills all in all.'[366]

Nevertheless, Taylor believed that even with this awareness, people tended to push the High God back, far out of reach, so that this God is considered only when the ancestors have failed. Much more real in daily life is interaction with the unseen world in dreams, or fear induced by the ill will of fellow human beings, easily associated with witchcraft. Taylor emphasises that in many African societies it is to this kind of paralysing fear, the dark side of African life, that the Gospel can bring liberating joy, a contrast from the Western version of freedom from sin. The breaking up of social harmony by antagonisms or evil intent, social and spiritual, causes dysfunction and death. 'The good news,' he wrote, 'consists first in the fact that the dominion of this gentle Lord is total. There are no strangers and no realms of terror that lie beyond his sovereignty.'[367] Christ as light is the antidote to the heart of darkness.

---

[364] Taylor, *Primal Vision*, pp. 74-75.
[365] Taylor, *Growth of the Church in Buganda*, p. 214.
[366] Taylor, *Primal Vision*, pp. 83, 84.
[367] Ibid., p. 193.

Church Missionary Society

In discussing Taylor's final major books, I shall dwell less on his time as general secretary of CMS, partly because I wrote an article in an earlier issue of the IBMR on his newsletters of 1963-75.[368] The newsletters reveal his strong condemnation of the Vietnam War, which he called 'shameful and futile,' and an emphasis on small groups and missionary cells to provide dynamism. The history of CMS itself, with its beginnings in a group of enthusiasts, reveals this emphasis, which Taylor referred to as 'God's arithmetic' – whether with Gideon in Judges 7 or in small groups in Uganda that Terry Waite, later a famous hostage in Beirut, was training to help the church forward. Taylor wrote, 'if we want men of stature, we should remember that they have always grown better in coteries of friends than structures of efficiency.'[369] Whether in the organisational sphere or the economic, Taylor was clearly attracted by the 'small is beautiful' message of E.F. Schumacher, also writing at this time.[370] Small groups can be 'cells of defiance,' a chapter title in a later book, against prevailing powers and cultural pressures; the small, the personal, and the spontaneous should be valued over against mere size of organisation. Mission should not be seen as only numerical growth. Rather, it is about the quality of life and its victory over evil. 'Numerical growth,' Taylor wrote, 'is not unimportant, for it is often an indication of the obedience or disobedience of the church...but God's arithmetic is more with representative numbers, the few who stood in for the many.'[371]

The tension of the few and the many, the small cell's dynamism against the large organisation, can be added to other tensions in his thinking. At Uppsala in 1968, when mainstream thinking of the

---

[368] Timothy Yates, 'Newsletter Theology,' *IBMR* 12 (1988): 11-15; *Supra*, Ch. 6.

[369] John V. Taylor, *CMS Newsletter*, no. 334 (September 1974). Taylor wrote elsewhere, 'I do not put my trust in the big battalions' (*Enough is Enough* [London: SCM Press, 1975], p. 87).

[370] E.F. Schumacher, *Small is Beautiful: A Study of Economics as if People Mattered* (London: Blond & Briggs, 1973).

[371] John V. Taylor, *For All the World* (London: Hodder & Stoughton, 1966), p. 83.

World Council of Churches was moving in the direction of social revolution as the way for mission and when conservative evangelical participants like Donald McGavran and John Stott were pleading for the traditional emphasis on the unevangelised and their conversion, Taylor stood between these 'verticalists', with their stress on God's dealing with the unconverted through the Gospel of salvation, and the 'horizontalists', who looked for a salvation mediated through revolutionary social movements. In Norman Goodall's report of the Uppsala Assembly, Taylor was described (as also D.T. Niles) as anxious to hold together 'the gospel of personal conversion and the gospel of social responsibility,'[372] which threatened to fly apart in the debate. Taylor, participating in the section 'Renewal and Mission,' found himself acting as a reconciling figure between the two strands. In an earlier book, *For All the World* (1966), he showed his firm commitment to what he called the threefold cord of mission: proclamation, witness and service – 'neither confusing them nor excluding any one of them because the three must be intertwined in mission.' Equally, his disillusionment with the old-style gospel of the 1930s is clear in this book – that is, any idea that we can build the kingdom by human effort rather than receiving it as God's gift.[373]

Taylor's newsletters, as also his First Lambeth Interfaith Lecture (1977), addressed interfaith issues and disagreed with John Hick as to the possibility of religious common ground and so a common speech religiously, which made it very difficult to generalise. Taylor wanted both to hold fast to the uniqueness and universality of Christ and to remain open and sensitive to others and to the Holy Spirit, so that 'pluralism' became an opportunity for God to bring about what Taylor liked to term 'exchange'; for, he wrote, every religion is 'a people's particular tradition of response to the reality which the Holy Spirit of God has set before their eyes.'[374]

---

[372] Norman Goodall, ed., *The Uppsala Report* (Geneva: WCC Publications, 1968), p. 24.
[373] Taylor, *For All the World,* pp. 41, 85, 88.
[374] John V. Taylor, *CMS Newsletter,* no. 303 (April 1967); John V. Taylor, 'The Theological Basis of Interfaith Dialogue' (the First

Finally, in this period we must note a prophetic book written in 1975 just before Taylor became a bishop. Entitled *Enough is Enough*, it drew on his CMS experiences around the world. For Western Europeans or North Americans, this book makes for very uncomfortable reading. It is a searing indictment of excess by the wealthy developed communities at the expense of poorer nations in terms of pollution of the planet, the exploitation of natural resources, and the false values of advertising. It is a cry to set limits, to reverence life, and to attend to the biblical emphasis on the personal. If he were asked 'Enough for what?' his reply would be 'Enough for the personal.'[375]

Doctrinal Writing, 1972-2001

Strictly, Taylor's 1972 book on the Holy Spirit belongs to his time at CMS, but I am handling it here with his other doctrinal writings. In 1975 he became bishop of Winchester and, in time, chairman of the Church of England's Doctrine Commission. This responsibility produced a report, *Believing in the Church*, under his chairmanship in 1981. In his introduction Taylor wrote of the excessive individualism of modern understanding of religious belief and its privatisation. By contrast, he wanted to emphasise that Christian believing and that of other communities, including, for instance, scientific researchers, was 'mainly belonging.' He quoted a book by the scientist John Ziman called *Public Knowledge* (1968) on 'the social dimension of science' (part of its subtitle) about this aspect. Research scientists were also part of a community: the community of science.

We turn to Taylor's own major books on the Godhead: *The Go-Between God* (1972) and *The Christlike God* (1992). The former went through thirteen impressions between 1972 and 1989, which suggests that it touched a theological nerve. In it Taylor presents a view of the Holy Spirit as one who primarily creates an intense *awareness* of God, of Christ, of one another, and as one who also creates a deep *communion*. As the 'in-between-God,' who creates

---

Lambeth Interfaith Lecture), in *Christianity and Other Religions*, ed. John Hick and Brian Hebblethwaite (London: Collins, 1980), p. 217.
[375] Taylor, *Enough is Enough*, p. 93.

awareness and communion, he is the one who opens eyes to reality, but of whom we are often not directly aware because he is 'in-between,' creating awareness of the other rather than drawing attention to himself.[376] Insofar as we see the Spirit revealed supremely in the life of Jesus Christ, he is shown to be the one who demands choice, as Jesus did of those around him; he also inspires sacrifice and self-oblation. Taylor does not apply this point only to persons. He followed Sir Alister Hardy, who, as a scientist, spoke in his Gifford Lectures of an element of choice even in inanimate chains of being in the universe. Taylor developed this point in describing the created universe as a whole being drawn toward a 'greater complexity and sensitiveness.'[377] The creative spirit is pressing the whole order of being in the twin directions of choice and life through death. In relation to the church, Taylor quoted Bonhoeffer in saying that 'the Church is nothing but a section of humanity in which Christ has really taken form,' the arena where the Spirit creates 'a new degree of communal awareness of the reality of Jesus Christ' as well as a 'new sensitiveness toward other people.'[378] Pentecostals had been right to stress that the Holy Spirit 'transforms and intensifies the quality of human life,' but Taylor thinks that this movement is chiefly to be realised in small groups, the 'little congregations' characterised by the four aspects of reflection, service, worship, and evangelism.[379] The two or three gathered together will realise this mutual awareness and communion, which is the gift of the Spirit, and they will have his openness to one another and to the world in need. This 'one another' (Greek *allēlōn*) is emphasised again and again in the New Testament in such texts as 'bear one another's burdens' and is a sign of the Spirit binding together those like Peter and Cornelius, who do not naturally belong together. Like Sir Arthur Eddington, Taylor wants to stress the 'and' in the assertion that 'one and one makes two' – here is the essential link between the one and the other, the 'and' where the Go-Between-God is to be found. The

---

376 John V. Taylor, *The Go-Between God* (London: SCM Press, 1972), p. 43.
377 Ibid., p. 107.
378 Ibid., pp. 107, 201.
379 Ibid., pp. 199, 148.

bond, which he calls 'the current of communication,' is both personal and invisible. Christians naturally call this 'Go-Between' The Holy Spirit.[380]

Between this fine book and his final major publication, Taylor wrote a shorter book, *Kingdom Come* (1989). Here he has good things to say about the kingdom of God and its right understanding. He reveals himself as a very competent biblical theologian.

Taylor's final book was *The Christlike God*, whose title was prompted by Michael Ramsey's aphorism 'God is Christlike, and in him is nothing unChristlike at all.' Taylor brought together his knowledge of patristic writings, Aristotle and Greek philosophy, and Thomas Aquinas with his wide reading in Old Testament scholarship and in modern systematicians like Hans Küng and Karl Rahner. Many other writers were called in, from William Wordsworth to Emily Brontë to Charles Williams, in order to answer the question, 'Why do so few really ask questions about the nature of God?' Taylor started from a simple question of a child, 'Is God always with us?' 'Yes, he is always there.' 'Doesn't he ever go to see the Murphys?' Taylor went on to expressions of the awareness of God in poets like Edith Sitwell and Edwin Muir and by a number of individuals who had communicated their experiences of God to Sir Alister Hardy's research team, when the doors of perception had been opened and an intense awareness of God had resulted.[381] Taylor contrasted the God of the covenant with common misunderstandings of God in the European tradition, which viewed God as a simple monad (pp. 119-24), as unchangeable (pp. 124-29), or as unaffected and impassible (pp. 135-39). In Taylor's view, it was better to speak of God's absolute freedom to be what he is or, with Austin Farrer, to speak of him in terms of the almightiness of love (p. 140). Taylor faced head-on the issues of theodicy raised by the Holocaust, the Gulag, Dachau, and Auschwitz, and the divine responsibility (pp. 198-205),

[380] Ibid., p. 17.
[381] John V. Taylor, *The Christlike God* (London: SCM Press, 1992), pp. 38-45.

presenting a vision of God who 'still believes the outcome will outweigh the immense waste and agony' and who calls us to believe in his staggering, costly venture, even while there is little evidence of its ever succeeding. He quoted a comment of Andrew Elphinstone about the cross as love making amends to those who feel that they cannot forgive God for all their pains. The theodicy offered took the deep pain of the world with seriousness but also warned that human shrinking from pain can mask a deliberate preference for being only half alive. As in the book on the Holy Spirit, the call to sacrifice – what Taylor calls here 'the cross at the heart of creation' – is the price of full human potentiality, as modelled in Jesus Christ.[382] This book is a tougher read than *The Go-Between God*, but it contains many good things, a remarkable product of Taylor's seventies. The chapter 'God Saw that It Was Good: The Cost of Creation' is particularly worthy of note.

Conclusion
In a series of addresses given in 1986 at the University of Oxford, published as *A Matter of Life and Death* (1986), Taylor gave expression to a theme that those who knew him well tell us was a constant refrain. 'Most people' he would say, 'are content to remain only half alive.' God is not 'hugely concerned as to whether we are religious or not. What matters to God, and matters supremely, is whether we are alive or not. If your religion brings you more fully to life, God will be in it; but if your religion inhibits your capacity for life or makes you run away from it, you may be sure God is against it, just as Jesus was.'[383] Part of being alive for Taylor was grappling with tensions. In the opening of his book on the Buganda, he quoted a Roman Catholic missiologist who had contrasted the Protestant Alexander Mackay's view of conversion as a 'psychological act of trust' with the Catholic emphasis on 'the inauguration of the candidate in the visible church.' Taylor would surely have said *both-and* to this tension of an individual act of faith and the 'corporate believing' noted above. Again, in his early book on politics in Africa, Taylor was not decrying the need for

---

382 Ibid., pp. 205, 204, 201, 203.
383 John V. Taylor, *A Matter of Life and Death* (London: SCM Press, 1986), p. 18.

133

the fervent spirituality of the revival brethren in East Africa but calling on such Christians to combine devotion with an attitude to politics that did not see it as staining the soul. In *Primal Vision* he wanted to combine the European stress on the cerebral with the African recognition of the instinctive; at CMS he emphasised the voluntary, the spontaneous, the small against size, organisation, and structures, without discounting the need for the latter but preferring the development of persons over structures of efficiency. In WCC circles he espoused equally the cause of the social movement urged by some 'horizontalists' and the emphasis on conversion and evangelism of the unreached upheld by the 'verticalists.'

In his books on doctrine Taylor wanted to combine structured understanding with Christian experience,[384] perhaps the secret of the enormous success of *The Go-Between God*, which also came out at a time of widespread interest in the Holy Spirit. His grappling with tensions was noticed in an appreciation after his death by his successor at CMS, Simon Barrington-Ward.[385] Max Warren, his predecessor at CMS, wrote of Taylor to his daughter in a letter of April 26, 1973, 'He is head and shoulders spiritually and mentally above any of his contemporaries and is one of the few Anglicans with a capacity for seeing six feet in front of his nose and then a little more. What is more, he doesn't possess the peculiar Anglican ecclesiastical squint which gets virtually every important issue out of focus.'[386] It has to be hoped that, as this article is written by a fellow Anglican, such impairment of vision has been avoided and that a fair portrait has emerged of Taylor as man and missiologist of stature in the twentieth century. He died in Oxford on January 30, 2001.

---

[384] Taylor, 'My Pilgrimage,' p. 61.
[385] Simon Barrington-Ward, *CMS 'Yes,'* April-June 2001, p. 20.
[386] Quoted in Graham Kings, 'Mission and the Meeting of Faiths: The theologies of Max Warren and John V. Taylor,' in *The Church Mission Society and World Christianity, 1799-1999*, ed. Kevin Ward and Brian Stanley (Grand Rapids: Eerdmans, 2000), pp. 304-5. This paper was a lecture at Asbury Theological Seminary in May 2011 and was published in *IBMR*, Vol. 30, No. 3, July 2006, pp.153-6.

CHAPTER 10

DAVID BOSCH: South African Context, Universal Missiology – Ecclesiology in the Emerging Missionary Paradigm

I begin this article about David Bosch (1929-1992) with a personal reminiscence. My first experience of a meeting of the International Association for Mission Studies (IAMS) was in Harare in 1985, at a time when Zimbabwe seemed to have thrown off the colonial yoke and was moving toward a fully integrated society, while South Africa was still experiencing apartheid. David Bosch and others had driven up from Pretoria to participate in the conference. I read a paper on Anglican Evangelical missiology that concentrated on the writings of Max Warren and Stephen Neill. Bosch showed great interest, with a certain theological anxiety at some of Max Warren's ideas on the cosmic Christ, but it was a good session with much participation. I discovered later that Bosch was suffering from a severe toothache. He nevertheless arranged to meet me later to talk missiology, a conversation that went on for two hours of highly stimulating discussion, even while he held his jaw in much pain. This incident illustrates the man and his commitment to truth through dialogue and to wholehearted engagement, irrespective of extreme personal discomfort.

Bosch the Afrikaner
Like all of us, David Bosch was a child of his own time and place. He was born into an Afrikaner farming family and baptised into membership of the Dutch Reformed Church (DRC).[387]

---

[387] J. Kevin Livingston, 'the Legacy of David J. Bosch,' *International Bulletin of Missionary Research* 23 (1999) pp.26-27. In what follows I am greatly indebted to Livingston's doctoral dissertation of 1989 for the University of Aberdeen, 'A Missiology of the Road: The theology of Mission and Evangelism in the writings of David Bosch,' 2 Vols. See also his essay 'David Bosch: An Interpretation of Some Main Themes in His Missiological Thought,' in *Mission in Creative Tension: A Dialogue with David Bosch*, ed. J.N.J. Kritzinger and W.A. Saayman (Pretoria: Southern African Missiological society, 1990), pp. 2-16.

Churchgoing was a serious matter for the family, involving travelling long distances on Saturdays and considerable efforts on Sundays. It is important to remember that he remained a member of the DRC for his whole life, despite latterly being effectively deprived of any preaching ministry within it. The DRC was the main repository of Afrikaans culture and tradition, forged in the nineteenth century into an identity over against the British and by such historical turning points as the Battle of Blood River of 1838, when 400 Boers formed a *laager*, or circle of ox wagons, against 10,000 Zulus; and by the Great Trek, whereby many Boers left the Cape to form the Transvaal across the Orange River and so escape British dominance. The DRC was Calvinist in its theology, anti-British in outlook, and racist in viewing blacks as inferior. During the nineteenth century, when Dutch Reformed clergy from Holland were scarce, the DRC in the Cape reinforced their numbers with Reformed clergy from Scotland, among them Andrew Murray. He was representative of a pietist, evangelical strand of Scottish church life, an injection of something of a rather different spirituality to the DRC that brought greater missionary awareness to the church. Much of the missionary life and vitality of the DRC can be traced to this source; in time David Bosch himself imbibed this influence.[388]

The war between the Boers and the British of 1899-1902, in which the British employed scorched-earth tactics against the Boer farmers and interned their families in concentration camps and during which 25,000 women and children died, hardened Afrikaner attitudes and gave added determination in the twentieth century to resist attempts to Anglicise their *volk*. In Bosch's early days, the DRC could be described as the Nationalist Party at prayer. The party, led by D.F. Malan and later by Hendrik Verwoerd, achieved political power in South Africa in the 1940s. In 1948 it enacted three pieces of legislation that enshrined apartheid as a political system: the Race Classification Act, the Group Areas Act, and the Mixed Marriages Act. The so-called homelands were set up eleven years later in 1959, under the Bantu Self-Government Act.

---

[388] Livingston, 'Missiology of the Road,' Vol. 1, pp. 110-111.

As far back as 1829 the DRC had refused to discriminate against black Africans in services of Holy Communion. Gradually, however, approaches to different ethnic groups, which were essentially practically based, were accorded theological justification. One unfortunate constituent of this discrimination was the German Lutheran teaching of Gustav Warneck of what might be called ethnic missiology.[389] What might be a fruitful approach to tribal mission in the hands of such people as Bruno Gutmann and Christian Keysser could also be employed by others to reinforce a fatal ethnic separation, in which black Africans could be treated as a separate ethnic *volk* rather than integrated into a racially diverse church fellowship. This potential does much to explain Bosch's later criticisms of both Warneck and of Donald McGavran for his 'homogeneous unit principle.'

Bosch and Apartheid

Bosch's personal career during these years of increasing dominance by the National Party included doctoral study under Oscar Cullmann in Basel in the 1950s. Bosch described to Kevin Livingston in an interview how, despite sharing the general Afrikaner rejoicing at the triumph of the National Party in 1948 ('a dream come true'), his attitude toward black Africans had begun to change as he organised services for farm workers as one intending to become a DRC minister: 'Previously I only thought of them as pagans and at best semi-savages…from then on I accepted Blacks as full human beings.'[390] It was a major discovery to find black Anglicans, Methodists, and African Independent Christians in the local black community. While studying in Basel, with the help of a fellow Afrikaner also in Europe for study, he found himself breaking with the whole ideology of apartheid.[391] In 1957 he returned to South Africa to work as a missionary among the Xhosa people (1957-67), during which time his mastery of the language became legendary in the way that Lesslie Newbigin's was of Tamil

---

389 For G. Warneck, C. Keysser, and B. Gutmann, see T. Yates, *Christian Mission in the Twentieth Century* (Cambridge: Cambridge Univ. Press, 1994), pp. 34-56.
390 Livingston, 'Legacy of David J. Bosch,' p. 26.
391 Livingston. 'Missiology of the Road,' Vol. 1, p.58.

in India. His period as missionary in the Transkei caused him to knit together missiology and *praxis*. Frans Verstraelen, a penetrating critic of Bosch's theology, has written of this period that it showed 'convincingly...his integrity as a human being...a Christian and as a missiologist.'[392] It was the time also when he gained experience of ecumenical life through the Transkei Council of Churches, where DRC members, Methodists, Roman Catholics, and others showed him the value of unity in action.

His time in the Transkei confirmed his shift in attitudes toward both Africans and the white paternalism then prevalent. One illustration of this was his observation of an African mechanic. While Bosch was standing over him, the man was incapable of mending his car, but later, left to himself, proved perfectly competent.[393] Bosch had not, like Beyers Naudé, been a member of the Afrikaner Broederbond and, confronted by events like the Sharpeville shooting of civilians by the police in 1960, did not experience the depth of rejection of Beyers Naudé in his repudiation – set out in a famous sermon of 1962 – of the Broederbond and DRC attitudes.[394] Nevertheless, after a short period teaching in a small seminary in the Transkei (1967-72), Bosch accepted a chair at the University of South Africa (UNISA) in Pretoria with much trepidation, knowing that to do so was to distance himself further from DRC theologians who looked on the faculty with suspicion; because of its large number of external students, the university had retained a mixed-race constituency.

As the 1970s advanced, Bosch's critical stance toward apartheid became stronger. In 1979 he chaired the South African Christian Fellowship Assembly, an important conference attended by 5,000 Christians over ten days with black Africans present, for which

---

[392] Frans J. Verstraelen, 'Africa in David Bosch's Missiology: Survey and Appraisal,' in *Mission in Bold Humility: David Bosch's Work Considered*, ed. Willem Saaymann and Klippies Kritzinger (Maryknoll, N.Y.: Orbis Books, 1996), p. 10.
[393] Livingston, 'Missiology of the Road,' Vol. 1, p59 n. 25.
[394] International Commission of Jurists, Geneva, *The Trial of Beyers Naudé: Christian Witness and the Rule of Law* (London: Search Press, 1975).

permission by the government was uncertain up to the start of proceedings. He stood out against violence as a method of achieving political change, believing that the stand he took had been the way of Jesus and that for the church to adopt violence was to adopt the ways of the world and ultimately to make itself redundant as a witness.[395] In the 1980s he was a leading figure in the *Ope Brief* (Open Letter) of 1982, signed by a large number of sympathetic ministers, that sought a change of heart among the leaders of the DRC, and in 1983 he contributed to a book of essays edited by John de Gruchy and Charles Villa Vicencio. The overall title was *Apartheid Is a Heresy*, and Bosch's piece was entitled 'Nothing but a Heresy.' For him, the issue was that identity in terms of race was being preferred to the common identity given to all people in the church, basically the same protest that Karl Barth and others had raised in the Barmen Declaration against acquiescence by the 'German Christians' to Nazi pressure to 'aryanise' the church and to expel Jewish Christians from the ministry. So to elevate race was to act heretically.

This background of personal struggle from a position of shared Afrikaner attitudes on racial issues in his early years to costly opposition after his return from Europe in 1957, especially in the UNISA years after 1972, is important as a background as Bosch's theology is assessed. In John Mackay's distinction between the 'balcony' and the 'road,' between the detached observer with his or her love of universals and ideas and the active participant, Bosch is undoubtedly (as Livingston called him) 'a missiologist on the road,' one of whose early writings on the relevance of Paul to missionary theory and practice was entitled *A Spirituality of the Road* (1979). He preferred to remain in 'prophetic solidarity' with the DRC, even when effectively banned in the 1970s from its pulpits, rather than repudiate his fellow Afrikaner Christians; but equally, given the opportunity to leave South Africa for a chair at

---

395 Livingston, 'David Bosch,' pp. 14-15, quoting Bosch, *Theologia Evangelica*, 'The Church in South Africa' 9 (July-September 1976) pp. 2-3. Bosch distanced himself from the Kairos Document of 1986 on the same grounds.

Princeton Theological Seminary, he refused to retreat to what could have been for him an academic balcony.

Critique of Bosch's Thought

Before narrowing this treatment to the theme of ecclesiology, we must face some of the criticisms of Bosch's corpus. Frans Verstraelen wrote a penetrating critique in the composite work *Mission in Bold Humanity*.[396] It must be conceded that Bosch's theology stands in the classical tradition of ideas 'from above' and so contrasts sharply with the liberation theologians' concentration on *praxis* and concrete contextualisation. Bosch himself conceded this point and was unapologetic about it,[397] but he recognised that *praxis* had its place with *theoria*, and in the interests of a human and theological holism he added a third aspect, *poiesis*, the need for a satisfying theological and missiological approach to provide beauty and worship. The same criticism was made in essence (and with special pointedness) when John de Gruchy and M.L. Daneel regretted the absence of Bosch's own missionary experience in the book *Witness to the World* (1980),[398] a work about which Orlando Costas also noted the absence of Third World Theology.[399]

Pentecostalism is indeed generally absent, as Willem Saayman noted,[400] and there is little reference to the contribution of women to mission, as discerned by Dana Robert.[401] Kirsteen Kim has suggested that Bosch's approach to the Holy Spirit is more modern

---

[396] Verstraelen, 'Africa in David Bosch's Missiology,' pp. 8-39.

[397] David J. Bosch, *Transforming Mission: Paradigm Shifts in Theology of Mission* (Maryknoll, N.Y.: Orbis Books, 1991), pp. 425, 431.

[398] Livingston, 'Missiology of the Road,' Vol. 1, p. 167 n.; see also p. 95.

[399] Orlando E. Costas, review of *Witness to the World*, by David Bosch, *International Review of Mission* 70, no. 278 (1981), pp. 82-86, especially at p. 83.

[400] Willem Saayman, 'A South African Perspective on *Transforming Mission*,' in *Mission in Bold Humility*, ed. Saayman and Kritzinger, p. 51.

[401] Dana L. Robert, 'American women and the Dutch Reformed Missionary Movement, 1874-1904,' in *Mission in Bold Humility*, ed. Saayman and Kritzinger, p. 94.

than postmodern: Bosch showed himself aware that the Orthodox view of the procession of the Spirit enabled them to view other religious traditions more positively, but it remains uncertain whether he would have followed this approach. It is more likely that he would have seen the Spirit tied more closely to the person of Christ, as in the Western tradition.[402] Nearer to our central theme, W. Nicol accused Bosch of a Docetic ecclesiology: his exposure to the kind of *Heilsgeschichte* views of a theologian like Oscar Cullmann, where salvation is contained within the church and sacred history is detached from the general historical continuum, allied to his espousal of the church as an 'alternative community,' a tendency that owed much to J.H. Yoder and Mennonite/Anabaptist views of the church, could on this view lead to a church withdrawn from the world. Even his frequent use of the term 'the Church' could be seen as a retreat into universals from the more messy business of dealing with actual ecclesial entities like the DRC. Against this criticism must be set Bosch's actual record of 'prophetic solidarity' as outlined above.[403]

Bosch on the Church vis-à-vis Mission

What, then, of Bosch's approach to ecclesiology and mission? First and foremost he held that the church was essential to Christian mission.[404] He turned to well-known authorities in Karl Barth, the documents of Vatican II, L.A. Hoedemaker, and Emil Brunner[405] to distinguish his position sharply from, for example, that of J.C. Hoekendijk, who bypassed the church for the world as central for

---

[402] Kirsteen Kim, 'Postmodern Mission: A Paradigm Shift in David Bosch's Theology of Mission?' *International Review of Mission* 89, no. 353 (2000), pp. 172-79.

[403] W. Nicol, 'The Cross and the Hammer: comparing Bosch and Nolan on the Role of the Church in Social Change,' in *Mission in Creative Tension*, ed. Kritzinger and Saayman, pp. 93-98; on 'church,' see Verstraelen, 'Africa in David Bosch's Missiology,' pp. 26-27.

[404] Bosch, *Transforming Mission*, p. 416; see also p. 386.

[405] David J. Bosch, *Believing in the Future: Towards a Missiology of Western Culture* (Valley Forge, Pa.: Trinity Press International, 1995), pp. 31-32.

mission.[406] In contrast, the section of Bosch's guide to mission theology is headed 'The Indispensability of the Church.'[407] In fairness to Hoekendijk, after the legitimate ecclesiocentric stress of Tambaram 1938, theology had felt the influence of the *Heilsgeschichte* school in which critics felt that God's work had been confined to salvation through the church. Against such a ghettoising tendency, Hoekendijk represented a violent reaction. In his writing, the church became marginalised,[408] while the true *missio Dei* took place in the world, as expressed in the phrase 'the world sets the agenda.' This tendency was marked at Uppsala 1968. Bosch, rightly in my view, while never identifying the church with the kingdom of God, saw it as the divinely given agent of mission, with the kind of interdependency between agency and mission that Brunner described when he famously noted, 'The church lives by mission as a fire lives by burning.'

As Bosch set his face against any marginalisation of the church in mission, so he opposed ethnic approaches (*Volkskirche*) as advocated by Warneck and worked out by Gutmann and Keysser. Bosch's *Sitz im Leben* is important here. What might be legitimate attempts to incorporate ethnic and cultural aspects of people like the Chagga (Gutmann) and the Kate (Keysser) in the manner sketched out by Warneck, was used by Afrikaner theologians to bolster a separate ethnic approach to black Africans which denied the catholicity of a mixed-race congregation and became for Bosch 'totally incompatible' with the community of Jesus. The Reformed Heidelberg Catechism asserted the church is at all times and in all places the one people of God gathered from the whole human race by Jesus Christ through the Holy Spirit and the Word (answer 54).

---

[406] David J. Bosch, *Witness to the World: the Christian Mission in Theological Perspective* (Atlanta: John Knox Press, 1980), pp. 176-77; For Johannes Christian Hoekendijk, see Hoekendijk's *Church Inside Out,* ed. L.A. Hoedemaker and Pieter Tijmes (London: SCM Press, 1967); and Yates, *Christian Mission in the Twentieth Century*, pp. 53-56.
[407] Bosch, Guide 1, MSR 201, 'Theology of Mission' (UNISA, 1975), p. 155.
[408] For Hoekendijk, ecclesiology is 'not more than a single paragraph in Christology' (Bosch, *Witness to the World*, pp. 176-77).

Ethnicity, discerned by Warneck in the *panta ta ethnē* (all the peoples) of Matthew 28:18-20, was a cultural and ethnic but not a theological category.[409] For Bosch, the same fatal tendency to elevate ethnicity at the expense of catholicity was present in Donald McGavran's writings. In Bosch's view, McGavran's obsession with numbers of converts obscured the greater need for catholicity. Again, one must enter a caution. The so-called 'homogeneous unit principle' of McGavran, as I have argued elsewhere,[410] was aimed at initial evangelistic practice. McGavran held that people of a specific race or social class were reached best in their own contexts, a case proved again and again in my view. But that statement in no way justifies postconversion segregation, when the principle of catholicity will assert itself in the convert, a point which McGavran did not dispute. For Bosch, however, sensitive to the consequences of an essentially pragmatic decision by the DRC in the 1820s to treat Africans separately, any subsequent attempt to justify segregation theologically on grounds of ethnicity was to be firmly resisted.

Marks of the Future Church

If Hoekendijk was to be confronted with the indispensability of the church in mission; Warneck, with the need for catholicity as overcoming ethnicity; and McGavran, with catholicity overcoming homogeneity, what marks of the church did Bosch wish to emphasise as crucial for its future witness? Once more, the context of the South African struggle can be discerned in what follows. First, *justice* must be an essential preoccupation. In the posthumously published monograph *Believing in the Future*, Bosch wrote of justice as 'what Christian are for' in a world where one-fifth of the entire world population lives in absolute poverty.[411]

---

409 Bosch in *Missionalia* 5, no. 2 (1977), p. 34; see P.J. Robinson, 'Mission as Ethics, Ethics as Mission, in *Mission in Creative Tension*, ed. Kritzinger and Saayman, pp. 164-65.
410 Bosch, *Witness to the World*, pp. 208-9; Yates, *Christian Mission in the Twentieth Century*, pp. 216-218.
411 Bosch, *Believing in the Future, pp.* 34, 37.

Christians must not divorce earthly justice and spiritual righteousness. They are closely related, if not identical.[412]

Second, *unity* must preoccupy the church. Bosch's experiences of practical ecumenism in the Transkei Council of Churches had shown the importance of unity in witness and action at the practical level, but this was a deeply held theological conviction also. Disunity is not 'just a vexation but a sin. Unity is not an optional extra...we should never tire of striving towards that day when Christians in every place may gather to share the One Bread and the One Cup.'[413] He had sought unity in the different branches of the Reformed family in the *Ope Brief* of 1982 and in the addresses of that year and in 1986 associated with unity.[414]

Third, the church must be a *reconciling community*. Although there was little in *Transforming Mission* on reconciliation, the emphasis on the church bringing both judgement and reconciliation was important to him,[415] and we may believe that the Truth and Reconciliation Commission in South Africa and Archbishop Desmond Tutu's Herculean efforts would have found a strong supporter in David Bosch.

Fourth, Bosch wanted to underscore that the church was *essentially* missionary. He endorsed Barth's view of the church as gathered, built up, and sent out, as he also did his view of the interaction of the church and mission as mutually life-giving. Bosch produced a catena of quotations in *Transforming Mission* from *Ad gentes*, Hoedemaker, Josef Glazik, Barth, and others to make the point with Friedrich Schleiermacher that 'the inverse of the thesis 'the

---

[412] David J. Bosch, 'The Scope of Mission' (CMS Annual Sermon, 1982), pp. 11-12; available through the archives of Crowther Centre for Mission Education, CMS, Oxford, England.
[413] Bosch, *Transforming Mission*, p.467.
[414] Livingston, 'David Bosch,' pp. 15-16.
[415] Livingston, 'Missiology of the Road,' Vol. 1, p. 71.

church is essentially missionary' is 'mission is essentially ecclesial.''[416]

Next, Bosch wanted to emphasise the fully representative nature of the *local*: 'the church-in-mission is primarily the local church everywhere in the world.'[417] There is no conflict here, he held, with the church universal, for the church universal finds its truest expression in local churches. With J.H. Oldham, he knew that the local is real, and he endorsed Lesslie Newbigin's dictum that the only hermeneutic of the Gospel is a congregation of men and women who believe it and live by it. For witness to be credible, it must flow from a local worshiping community, and in the future church it will be the laity and their witness that will carry greater credibility than the 'guild of pastors.'[418]

Finally, the church must have *worship* at the centre of its life, and it must be an *eschatological* community. Bosch found Protestant ecumenical theology with its stress on involvement in the world reflected in the theology of Vatican II, 'so that it sometimes seems as if the Church as a worshipping community has faded away.'[419] Mission is 'moored in the Church's worship, to its gathering around the Word and the Sacraments.'[420] The church can give only what it has received from God.[421] People not only need truth and justice (*theoria, praxis*), 'they also need beauty, the rich resources of symbol, piety, worship, love, awe and mystery,' what he calls the dimension of *poiesis.*[422] Bosch gives an important place also to the church's intercession. The eschatological elements will mean

---

[416] Bosch, *Transforming Mission*, p. 372; Karl Barth, *Church Dogmatics* (Edinburgh: T&T Clark, 1956), 4.1, pp. 725-26; *Ad gentes*, sec. 9.
[417] Bosch, *Transforming Mission*, p.378.
[418] Bosch, *Believing in the Future*, p. 59.
[419] Bosch, *Witness to the World*, p. 185.
[420] Bosch, *Transforming Mission*, p.385.
[421] Bosch, Guide 1, 201, pp. 155-56.
[422] Bosch, *Transforming Mission*, p.431; for intercession, see Guide 1, MSR 201, p.157.

that the church is not simply tied to human programs but, in a world devoid of hope, will provide that vital constituent.[423]

Bosch and the Present and Future Church

In his final essay on missiology, Bosch recognised that new forms of church expressions were emerging. It would be in ecclesial forums like the German Kirchentag – which, Bosch noted, 140,000 young people had attended in Munich in 1984 – that some of the pressing issues of the world church were more likely to be considered than in the average Sunday morning congregation.[424] Ecclesiology provided the essential antidote to a world of post-Enlightenment individualism, which had spawned the voluntarist missionary societies as its missionary expression. Interdependence and the corporate were the counter to what he called 'the monomaniac rejection of the empirical church' by Hoekendijk and similar thinkers; 'without the church there can be no evangelism or mission' remained his view.[425]

David Bosch assumed the traditional marks of the church as one, holy, catholic, and apostolic. We have to ask: how far had his own version of these characteristics, as outlined above, provided for the future? The twenty-first century challenges the church at certain discernible points: globalisation would seem to imply that a world body will need to shape its responses to such global issues as consumerism, exploitation of natural resources, and threats to the planet itself with more than local and fragmented efforts. While we may wholeheartedly endorse his heavy emphasis on the local church, his lesser stress on the necessity for catholicity to be also expressed in larger units and networks will become of great importance. In terms of local congregations, I have written elsewhere that 'indigenous forms of Christianity which bear comparison to [Pentecostal groups] with their emphasis on healing,

---

[423] Bosch, *Transforming Mission*, pp. 387, 499; D.J. Bosch, 'The Church in South Africa – Tomorrow,' *Pro Veritate* 14, no. 4 (1975), pp. 4-6, and no. 5 (1975), pp. 11-13, abstracted in *Missionalia* 3, no. 3 (1975), p. 177.
[424] Bosch, *Believing in the Future*, pp. 45, 64 n. 10.
[425] Bosch, *Transforming Mission*, pp. 416-417.

prophecy and exuberant worship with speaking with tongues, have sprung up as independent, nondenominational expressions of local Christianity,'[426] referring in particular to Latin American and African Initiated local churches. In the twenty-first century a major challenge to a body like the World Council of Churches (WCC) is to connect with local expressions of Christianity and somehow offer them input and influence as the great issues are debated conciliarly, the alternative being a highly fragmented witness that risks being dissipated and ineffective. It is an issue that the Roman Catholic Church has had to address in regard to the Base Ecclesial Communities in Latin America.

Issues of ecology, alluded to above, were noticed by Kirsteen Kim as being absent from the Bosch corpus, but they made a late appearance in *Believing in the Future*. The twenty-first-century church, in line with Bosch's stress on justice, needs to hold world governments and their leadership to fairness in relation to the planet and the world economy. The contribution of Ulrich Duchrow to the IAMS conference at Buenos Aires in 1996 brought home the missiological nature of the economic challenges for the future.[427] The stewardship of the planet, which the WCC has taught us to refer to as the 'integrity of creation,' means that nations the size of the United States and China, with their potential worldwide impact on climate change and the environment, will need the constant witness of the church on behalf of the well-being of the human race, a witness likely to be fully effective only if it is in some sense united. Despite the twenty-first century's dislike of the large, the institutional, and the overarching in narrative, the church is committed to all three and cannot in responsibility deny them. A further inescapable issue of justice remains over the place accorded to women in human societies after a century that could be called their century, in terms of progress toward achieving equality in many realms of human endeavour. Once more, the twenty-first-century church has a role to play, while also wrestling internally with its own questions on the issue.

---

426 Yates, *The Expansion of Christianity*, p. 181.
427 Ulrich Duchrow, 'God or Mammon? Economies in Conflict,' *Mission Studies* 13 (1996), pp. 32-67.

Conclusion

David Bosch was a missiologist of great integrity, one who managed to integrate in himself (as Andrew Walls has written) 'the three public domains' of academia, the church, and wider society, 'dimensions of the same reality' involving 'the integration of intellectual rigour, particularly in the life of the church, and practical demonstration in the life of the world.'[428] As Walls wrote, the attempt brought him 'great discomfort,' but this was disregarded. I have deliberately omitted from this treatment his long struggle with different understandings of the Gospel as expressed by 'ecumenicals' and 'evangelicals' which he stated was the context for his widely read book *Witness to the World* (1980). Here as so often his overriding concern was for the truth of the Gospel, expressed as much in social action for the neighbour as in the proclamation of divine grace in Jesus Christ, with no priority to either. It was this same integrity that made him feel an evangelical at the WCC Commission on World Mission and Evangelism conference at Melbourne, and an ecumenical at the Lausanne conference at Pattaya, both held in 1980. Concern for the full truth of the universal Gospel would not permit him to let go of essential alternative insights. So we have a missiologist who was also a missionary, an ecumenical leader who was also an evangelical, a lifelong member of the DRC in critical solidarity with his Afrikaans roots who never repudiated his fellow Afrikaner Christians. In these and many other respects he may be judged to

---

[428] Andrew F. Walls, 'Missiologist of the Road: David Jacobus Bosch (1929-1992),' in *The Cross-Cultural Process in Christian History* (Maryknoll, N.Y.: Orbis Books, 2002), p. 274. Walls' article, a very valuable assessment, originally appeared in *Occasional Newsletter* (of the British and Irish Association for Mission Studies), no. 2, March 1994, pp. 1-5. After Bosch's death on April 15, 1992, the *International Review of Mission* printed a short obituary in 81, no. 323 (July 1992), p. 362. See also the appreciation by Willem Saayman and Klippies Kritzinger, Bosch's academic colleagues at UNISA, 'David Bosch, the South African,' in *Mission in Bold Humility*, ed. Saayman and Kritzinger, pp. 1-7.

have been a faithful witness to us of many nations other than South Africa, indebted as we are to this 'missiologist of the road.'[429]

[429] This paper was a contribution to the IAMS Conference at Port Jackson, Malaysia of 2004 and was subsequently published in *IBMR* Vol.33, No. 2, pp. 72-8 and in *Perspectives Missionnaires*, No, 59 (2010/1), pp. 21-36.

CHAPTER 11

LESSLIE NEWBIGIN'S MISSIONARY ENCOUNTER WITH THE ENLIGHTENMENT, 1975-98

Lesslie Newbigin (1909-98) and Stephen Neill (1900-84) were fellow workers for the World Council of Churches (WCC) in Geneva, as both were also missionaries in India and bishops. Both played important roles in the formation of the Church of South India (CSI) in 1947. Where Neill came from an Anglican background, Newbigin had trained for Presbyterian ministry but became a bishop in CSI at its inception.

This article is mostly concerned with the period after Newbigin's return to England from India in 1974. His life and missiology have attracted much interest. Before Newbigin died, George Hunsberger wrote *Bearing the Witness of the Spirit: Lesslie Newbigin's Theology of Cultural Plurality* (1998), which the subject regarded as a good account, although somewhat demurring at the idea that election was the key to his theology. The year 2000 saw the publication of two studies, Geoffrey Wainwright's *Lesslie Newbigin: A Theological Life* and Michael Goheen's *'As the Father Has Sent Me, I Am Sending You': J.E. Lesslie Newbigin's Missionary Ecclesiology*, and there has been a further set of essays edited by Thomas Foust, George Hunsberger, Andrew Kirk, and Werner Ustorf entitled *A Scandalous Prophet: The Way of Mission After Newbigin* (2002).[430] There is also an ongoing application of his theology to contemporary concerns in the Gospel and Culture program in both the United Kingdom and the United States, and a sister network in New Zealand, the Deep Sight Trust, aims to provide a complete and comprehensive bibliography of his writings at www.newbigin.net. We await the biographical work of Eleanor Jackson, fellow worker in the WCC and in India.

---

[430] See also Geoffrey Wainwright, 'Newbigin,' in *Biographical Dictionary of Evangelicals*, ed. Timothy T. Larsen (Downers Grove, Ill.: Intervarsity Press, 2003), pp. 472-75, which provides a particularly helpful short digest of his life and work.

Background, Preparation, and India Ministry

In this article, which concentrates on Newbigin's encounter with modernity and postmoderntiy after 1974, some background to the cluster of writings of that time can be provided by his autobiography *Unfinished Agenda* of 1985. He was born in Northumberland, England, to a ship-owning father. He went to a Quaker boarding school and to Queens' College, Cambridge. He seems to have arrived at the university as a thoughtful agnostic. He became drawn into the activity of the Student Christian Movement (SCM) but still described himself as 'interested but sceptical and basically unconvinced.' A fellow student, Arthur Watkins, football captain and deeply committed Christian, had much to do with Newbigin's move into Christian faith; 'he made me want to pray,' Newbigin wrote of Watkins. Newbigin had a formative experience when helping with a Quaker group, serving among the unemployed of a mining community in the Rhondda Valley in Wales; one night the men came back roaring drunk, and the young Newbigin was at a loss. His despair at their lot and his own inadequacy led to a vision of the cross 'spanning the space between heaven and earth, between ideals and present realities with arms which embraced the whole world.' He wrote: 'I was sure that night, in a way that I had never been before, that this was the clue which I must follow if I were to make any kind of sense of the world. From that moment I would always know where to begin again when I had come to the end of my own resources of understanding or courage.'[431]

By his second year at Cambridge Newbigin was already a reader of the *International Review of Missions*, but at that stage he had no thought of either ordination or missionary work. In the same year, however, at an SCM conference in Swanwick in Derbyshire, he had an experience of calling, against his previous intentions. 'There was a tent set aside for prayer. On an afternoon near the end of the week I went into it to pray…While I was praying something happened which I find it hard to describe. I suddenly knew that I had been told that I must offer for ordination. I had not been

---

[431] Lesslie Newbigin, *Unfinished Agenda: An Autobiography* (London: SPCK, 1985), pp. 10, 12.

thinking about this. But I knew that I had been ordered and that it was settled and that I could not escape.' He anticipated terrible disappointment in his father, whose only son and natural successor in business he had been, but his father never wavered: 'I must do what God called me to do,' he said; 'there was not the faintest hint of disappointment or reproach.'[432] At seventy, rather like Abraham, the father was capable of an act of great faith in his son.

Lesslie became an SCM representative in Scotland in 1931, trained for ordination at Westminster College, Cambridge (a Presbyterian college), between 1933 and 1936, and sailed for India in September 1936. By then, on his own account, his personal study of Paul's letter to the Romans, with the help of James Denney's commentary in the Expositor's Greek Testament series, had been as determinative of his theological outlook as the letter had been for Augustine, Martin Luther, and Karl Barth. In particular, Newbigin had added to his vision of the cross in Wales an equally clear understanding of the finished work of Christ as an objective atonement; he wrote, 'At the end of the exercise I was much more an evangelical than a liberal.'[433] He had also met Helen, daughter of Irish missionary parents, a graduate of the University of Edinburgh, also an SCM representative and already offering for missionary service. They married and then spent most of the period 1936-74 in India, with some painful periods of separation. Newbigin had a large role in the creation of CSI and became bishop of Madurai in 1947. He worked for the International Missionary Council between 1957 and 1965 and was largely responsible for the integration of IMC with the WCC, which took place finally after great debate at the New Delhi assembly of the WCC in 1961. From 1965 to 1974 he served in India as bishop of Madras in CSI.

Polanyi's Enlightenment Critique

By the time of his retirement in 1974, Newbigin was already an established theological writer, with books like *The Household of God* (1953) and *Honest Religion for Secular Man* (1966), to name

---

432 Ibid., pp. 15-16, 17.
433 Ibid., p. 31.

only two. More important for this article, he had digested works that were profoundly critical of the European Enlightenment, providing him with a range of issues that he was to address from 1974 until his death. Perhaps the most significant of the thinkers he was reading was the Hungarian professor of chemistry Michael Polanyi – in particular, his books *Personal Knowledge* and *The Tacit Dimension*. The first was a course of Gifford Lectures of 1951. In the preface of the published version of 1958 Polanyi wrote: 'I start by rejecting the ideal of scientific detachment...I want to establish an alternative ideal of knowledge' by which '*the personal participation* of the knower in all acts of understanding...does not make our understanding *subjective*. Comprehension is neither an arbitrary act nor a passive experience, but a responsible act claiming universal validity. Such knowing is indeed *objective* in the sense of establishing contact with a hidden reality...it seems reasonable to describe this fusion of the personal and the objective as Personal Knowledge.'[434]

Polanyi wanted to rebut 'scientism,' the exaltation of the empirical and the so-called neutral intelligence, by arguing that all discovery is based on 'fiduciary acts.' Scientists, for example, believe in order and believe that their inquiry will reveal aspects of an ordered universe. Polanyi returned to Augustine, where a fiduciary act is prior to discovery: *credo ut intelligam* (I believe in order that I may understand). Belief, Polanyi argued, is the source of all knowledge,[435] and he referred to books 1-9 of the *Confessions*.

In the 1950s Newbigin thus found in Polanyi a critique of Enlightenment presuppositions where all is brought to the bar of a supposedly neutral intelligence. Polanyi posed a different approach to epistemology, a more well-rounded theory of knowledge, where more than pure reason was involved and (a theme dear to Newbigin's heart) the pursuit of truth was a passionate one, expressed in personal commitment. For Polanyi, it is by personal commitment that we choose to rely on certain 'tools' and integrate

---

[434] Michael Polanyi, *Personal Knowledge: towards a Post-Critical Philosophy* (London: Routledge & Kegan Paul, 1974), pp. vii-viii.
[435] Ibid., p. 266.

them into an overall 'focal' awareness. He used the examples of the learning process of trial and error in learning to ride a bicycle or to swim, where doing and commitment are involved, not just pure thought. Such personal knowledge also has the advantage of avoiding the dangers of the detaching effects of analysis.[436]

Newbigin on the Enlightenment

The Other Side of 1984. By the time Newbigin came to write his first essay addressing the assumptions of the Enlightenment, in a booklet for the British Council of Churches entitled _The Other Side of 1984_ (1983), he had come (in company with the archbishop and philosopher William Temple) to the view that the direction taken by European thought following the Frenchman René Descartes – the way of radical scepticism, doubting everything except one's own thinking processes – had been a disaster. _Cogito ergo sum_ (I think, therefore I am) is essentially individualistic and makes the individual's reason supreme.

The Enlightenment developed a sharp division between fact and value: _facts_ are demonstrable, empirical, and verifiable, and are contrasted with _values_, which are open to debate, private, and unverifiable. The next stage was to say in the modern way, 'You have your truth, and I have mine.' Absolute truth is unattainable. This was a long way from the truth claims of 'universal intent' that he had found in Polanyi and was to apply to the Gospel. Enlightenment approaches to truth, as he saw them, had led to the disappearance of hope. He wrote of the England that he returned to in the 1970s: 'There is little sign among the citizens of this country of the sort of confidence in the future... [of] the earlier years of this century.' And, 'our civilisation has so completely lost confidence in its validity,' and that in the space of a generation.[437]

The so-called Enlightenment framework had proved inadequate: Kant's _sapere aude_ (dare to know) and 'have the courage to use your understanding' led to a form of understanding that no longer

[436] Ibid., pp. 61, 62-63.
[437] Lesslie Newbigin, _The Other Side of 1984: Questions for the Churches_ (Geneva: World Council of Churches, 1984), pp. 1, 3.

satisfied. Newbigin quoted Polanyi to the effect that the Enlightenment's 'incandescence' had 'fed on the combustion of the Christian heritage in the oxygen of Greek rationalism and the fuel was exhausted, the critical framework itself burnt away.' One crucial example offered is the way, under Enlightenment presuppositions (supplied in this instance by Adam Smith's 'invisible hand' in the realm of economics), that economics and ethics part company. William Blake, the visionary of the eighteenth and early nineteenth centuries, was right in judging that 'any sphere of human life which is withdrawn from the Kingship of Christ [has] fallen under another rule.'[438] For Blake it resulted in 'dark Satanic mills' (from his poem now known as the hymn 'Jerusalem'). Economics detached from Christ's lordship becomes satanic, not neutral or beneficial, proceeding placidly under the influence of an unseen hand.

Foolishness to the Greeks. In his 1986 book *Foolishness to the Greeks; The Gospel and Modern Culture*, which resulted from his B.B. Warfield Lectures at Princeton Theological Seminary in 1984, Newbigin returned to these themes. By withdrawing into a private sector, Christianity had indeed secured for itself a place to be, but it had surrendered the crucial field. He quoted William Gladstone, the prime minister of Victorian times, to the effect that in the Roman Empire Christianity presented itself to the state as a public faith and not as a subjective experience. As Newbigin viewed contemporary Britain, he saw a pagan society, one 'far more resistant to the gospel than the pre-Christian paganism.' In modern states, when the pursuit of happiness by the greatest number of citizens is the aim, such a teleology has replaced the ancient wisdom that the true aim of man is to glorify God: it offers only a this-worldly hope and so constitutes a vast change of outlook. A theologian like Friedrich Schleiermacher, who had encouraged a retreat into religious experience, may have provided

---

[438] Ibid., pp. 21, 11, 40.

a hiding place, but he had made no provision for challenging the public ideology of the culture.[439]

Today, Newbigin wrote, nothing less than a conversion of the mind is required, out of the West's generally accepted 'plausibility structures' (a phrase of Peter Berger's) to ones where 'the living God' is recognised, 'whose character is 'rendered' for us in the pages of Scripture.' The church will need the language of testimony, in the way that Jesus testified before Pilate, an encounter that demonstrated that truth-bearing is a public act and that the church, as a community of testimony bearing people, is never just a private society. There can be no return to the old post-Constantinian Christendom, but neither can the church 'go private.' To do so is 'in effect to deny the kingship of Christ over all life, public and private... to deny that Christ is the truth by which all other truth claims are tested.'[440]

Once more he returned to the economy. *Religion and the Rise of Capitalism* (1926), by Christian economist R.H. Tawney, had shown that both Luther and Calvin had asserted the government of God in the economic realm. Nevertheless, Newbigin was as suspicious of Islam's absolute identification of the law of the state with the law of God (the sacralising of politics) as he was of aspects of the Religious Right in the United States. Of both he wrote that 'the total identification of a political goal with the will of God always unleashes demonic powers.' In the Old Testament, the idolatry associated with the true religion of Yahweh is more dangerous than that associated with the Baals. In Christian understanding a state is needed that both acknowledges the Christian faith and 'deliberately provides full security for those of other views.' In realms like religious education, however, he believed that the state cannot be neutral, a view he brought to bear when used as a religious adviser on the Birmingham religious education syllabus and at odds with another adviser used, John

---

[439] Lesslie Newbigin, *Foolishness to the Greeks: The Gospel and Western Culture* (Grand Rapids: Eerdmans, 1986), pp. 17-20, 34-35, 45.
[440] Ibid., pp. 64 -65, 94, 100, 102.

157

Hick. Denominations, which had in the United Kingdom bedevilled efforts at religious education in schools earlier in the century, he viewed as leading to a fragmentation that was disastrous, causing the church to be unable to confront society as a whole. The need was 'to return again to the form of the Catholic church'; meanwhile, a body like the WCC was in his view indispensable.[441]

The Gospel in a Pluralist Society. How many writers will publish a book as penetrating and substantial as Newbigin's next major work, *The Gospel in a Pluralist Society* (1989), in their eightieth year? As a background to this remarkable achievement, two items that preceded it deserve notice, which appear in some talks Newbigin gave in Scotland. First, he told the story of his meeting with an Indonesian general in Bangkok in 1980 at a conference called Salvation Today. Newbigin had heard this man say *sotto voce* in a group meeting, 'Of course the question is: can the West be converted?' The second is a quotation from Carver Yu on the disintegration of the West, characterised, so Yu wrote, by 'technological optimism and literary despair.' The main book resulted once again from a course of lectures, this time at the University of Glasgow, the Alexander Robertson Lectures for 1988. Newbigin contrasted the call in the New Testament to proclaim the truth with the attitude of the contemporary church. The latter offers its beliefs 'as simply one of many brands available in the ideological supermarket,' by which approach it lacks the kind of offence that the truth of the Gospel seen as governing public life might give. He wanted by contrast to challenge the plausibility structures of post-Enlightenment society and make the resurrection the epistemological starting point, so that all reality is understood in its light. The tendency in modern society is to ask not whether religious belief is true or false but whether those who hold the belief are sincere. Newbigin returned to Polanyi for his approach to truth claims, but in doing so, he began to face up to the issues of postmodernism, where claims to truth are seen as manifestations of the will to power in the manner of Nietzsche. If the ontological basis for language is removed (i.e., its reference to

---

[441] Ibid., pp. 106-7, 116-17, 147.

agreed reality), then 'the language of values is simply the will to power wrapped up in cotton wool.' For Newbigin, the modern resort to 'what is true for me' is 'an evasion of the serious business of living...a tragic loss of nerve in our contemporary culture...a preliminary symptom of death.'[442]

We know from Wainwright's book that C.N. Cochrane's study of the break-up of the civilizations of Greece and Rome, *Christianity and the Classical Culture*, had influenced Newbigin at this point. Once the pursuit of truth as reality was surrendered and a kind of willed multiplicity entertained, syncretistic and polytheistic, civilization was doomed to decay.[443]

Newbigin quoted Jürgen Moltmann, who had written of the European literature that it is 'characterised by cold despair, loss of vision, resignation and cynicism.' This lack of hope, discerned by Newbigin as the context for the proclamation of the Gospel, had produced a world where 'it is difficult to find Europeans who have any belief in a significant future worth working for.' By contrast, faith enables people to be at the same time realistic and hopeful – realistic because we know that no human project can eliminate the powers of darkness, but hopeful because in 'doing resolutely that relative good which is possible now...we offer it to the Lord who is able to take it and keep it for the perfect kingdom which is promised.' He quoted Rheinhold Niebuhr: 'We have an absolute duty to choose the relatively better among possibilities, none of which is absolutely good.'[444]

Newbigin argued that it is an illusion of post-Enlightenment individualistic culture that the Gospel is addressed to the individual. Rather it is addressed to societies, nations, and cultures. Furthermore, it is a myth that human beings have to hear in the 'rarefied atmosphere of pure neutrality of the Enlightenment.'

442 Lesslie Newbigin, *Mission and the Crisis of Western Culture* (London: Handsel Press, 1989), pp. 1, 2, 7, 17, 22.
443 Wainwright, *Newbigin: A Theological Life*, p. 401; cf. p. 429 n. 67.
444 Lesslie Newbigin, *The Gospel in a Pluralist Society* (Grand Rapids: Eerdmans, 1989), pp. 91, 90, 114-115, 139.

Such modernity did not 'provide enough nourishment for the human spirit.' Pluralism in society is a fact, but when pluralism is accepted as a principle, then society becomes pagan, for it worships gods other than the true God a characteristic not of secularity but of paganism. In such a society, the congregation has to become the hermeneutic of the Gospel, providing public truth and giving coherence and direction to society. He wrote, 'The only hermeneutic of the gospel is a congregation of men and women who believe it and live by it.'[445]

Truth to Tell. Newbigin returned to these basic themes once more in a little book of 1991 called *Truth to Tell*. It can be seen both as a useful first way into his thought and also as a summation of it. Here again the emphasis is on the Gospel as public truth: the need for truth claims over against the loss of nerve in the West; the criticism of the Cartesian search for certainty by way of radical doubt as a dead end; the combination of objective discovery in science, for example, with subjective involvement as learned from Polanyi, so that all knowing is personal knowledge; the need to insist that the Gospel is not just 'true for us' but true universally; and the rejection of individualism in favour of 'a community of love,' which is 'the reality for which and from which all things exist' – so that the rejection of relatedness is fatal, for in relatedness lies the true road to freedom. Rejection of relatedness is demonstrable in Western society in the breakdown of marriage, the break-up of families, and the development of consumerism, 'where the free market is made into an absolute… [that] becomes a power which enslaves human beings.[446]

Newbigin in Perspective

Before proceeding to a conclusion, I want here to enter some cautions, based in part on the evaluative essays in *A Scandalous Prophet* and in part on my own reflections. The first caution is a fundamental issue: how far is Lesslie Newbigin's profile of the Enlightenment to be accepted as it stands? It is interesting to note that even Hendrik Kraemer, whom Newbigin admired greatly as a

---

445 Ibid., pp. 199, 212, 213, 220, 227.
446 Lesslie Newbigin, *Truth to Tell* (London: SPCK, 1991), p. 76.

man and writer, in his great book *The Christian Message in a Non-Christian World* conceded that the onset of the Enlightenment in Europe had a liberating effect on intellect and culture, for very long subject to the dominance of hierarchies and authorities, whether aristocratic or papal, civil or ecclesiastical. Kraemer admitted that the new approaches blew open the doors of an often stifling room and let in much-needed air and oxygen.[447] Andrew Walls, in his essay of assessment, admitted himself to be a son of the Scottish Enlightenment (and Scotland was the home of Adam Smith and David Hume, central figures of it) and makes the intriguing suggestion that Christianity used the Enlightenment syncretistically, much in the way of Clement of Alexandria and the early apologists with Hellenism, though Walls does not say this explicitly. He does, however, give the example of the Scots missionary Alexander Duff, of the nineteenth century in India, who is an outstanding example of such syncretism, putting equal weight on the Bible and on European learning as the way to convince educated and cultured Brahmins of the truth of the Christian faith. Walls cites Origen, who wrote of the Israelites using Egyptian gold to cover the tabernacle: 'There was a Christian appropriation of the Enlightenment which was not at all a betrayal of Christian faith. It was an indigenisation of Christianity in Western terms. It was syncretistic.'[448]

Walls accepted that Enlightenment presuppositions can be shown to be of little consequence, for example, to emerging African Christianity, where there is what he calls 'an open frontier between the natural and the supernatural worlds,' creating 'open spaces left vacant by the older theology.'[449] Although Newbigin saw the Enlightenment as the great enemy, the combination of evangelicalism and Enlightenment in someone like Duff produced a man 'absolutely confident as he faces the powers of India in a

[447] Hendrik Kraemer, *The Christian Message in a Non-Christian World* (London: Edinburgh House, 1938), p. 116.
[448] Andrew Walls, 'Enlightenment, Postmodernity, and Mission,' in *Scandalous Prophet: The Way of Mission after Newbigin*, ed. Thomas F. Foust, George R. Hunsberger, J. Andrew Kirk, and Werner Ustorf (Grand Rapids: Eerdmans, 2002), p. 150.
[449] Ibid., pp. 151, 150.

universe of knowledge of which the Bible is the centre and the sun and in which politics and economics and the natural sciences have their proper place that comes from the rational Calvinist model he had learned at St Andrews,' a reference to the ancient Scottish university. Possibly Newbigin himself had second thoughts on such negativity. Lynne Price, in her essay in the same work, tells us that at a late stage in the final draft of *The Other Side of 1984*, Newbigin introduced some paragraphs that were more positive about the definite gains of the Enlightenment, as removing 'barriers to freedom of conscience and intellectual enquiry.'[450]

As a second caution, I agree with Bert Hoedemaker that the kind of global Christianity that Newbigin sought and that resulted in the formation of the WCC in 1948, expressed also in the inauguration of CSI in 1947, looks today like a project based on modernity rather than on the postmodern understandings of the present. For myself, however, whatever the prevailing fashions, I believe that Newbigin's search for visible unity among Christians (which in CSI included a united church of Congregationalists, Methodists, Anglicans, and Presbyterians) was built on a true vision of the potential of a God-given unity across barriers – based, as he based it, on the High Priestly Prayer of John 17 and, as it can also be, on the Letter to the Ephesians. But I am aware that our generation, sceptical of large so-called metanarratives, is inclined to look askance at such overarching projects. This does not mean Newbigin's efforts were wrong, even if currently intellectually and spiritually unfashionable.

Geoffrey Wainwright in his helpful overview gives us chapter headings that well communicate Lesslie Newbigin's diverse contribution: confident believer, direct evangelist, ecumenical advocate, pastoral bishop, missionary strategist, religious interlocutor, and Christian apologist: all these he was.[451] One thing that comes through any assessment of his life is the exceptional

---

450 Lynne Price, 'Churches and Postmodernity: Opportunity for an Attitude Shift,' in *Scandalous Prophet*, ed. Foust et al., p. 107 n. 1; Newbigin, *The Other Side of 1984*, pp. 15-16.
451 Wainwright, *Newbigin: A Theological Life*, p. 392.

integration that he achieved of *evangelistic and pastoral engagement* and of *theological commitment*. Would that more in positions of Christian leadership could hold these two poles so well in creative tension!

I close with some words of Newbigin's own on conversion, from his excellent little book *The Open Secret* (1978), a splendid introduction to missiology for students of missiology: 'Conversion is to Christ. It is primarily and essentially a personal event in which a human person is laid hold of by the Living Lord Jesus Christ at the very centre of the person's being and turned toward him in loving trust and obedience... [To confess Jesus as Lord is possible] only because I have been laid hold of by Another and commissioned to do so. It is not primarily or essentially my decision. By ways that are mysterious to me, that I can only faintly trace, I have been laid hold of by one greater than I and led into a place where I must make this confession and where I find no way of making sense of my own life or of the life of the world except through being an obedient disciple of Jesus.'[452] He would want to say that it was by God's grace alone. We can add, however, that he became one of the outstanding disciples of Jesus Christ in the twentieth century and continues to challenge and inspire into the twenty-first.[453]

---

[452] Lesslie Newbigin, *The Open Secret: An Introduction to the Theology of Mission* (Grand Rapids: Eerdmans, 1995), pp. 139, 17; originally given as lectures in the University of Birmingham and its then School of Mission and first published in 1978. Newbigin also wrote an article 'Conversion,' in the *Concise Dictionary of the Christian World Mission*, ed. Gerald Anderson, John Goodwin, and Stephen C. Neill (London: Lutterworth, 1971), pp. 147-48.

[453] This paper was a lecture at the School of World Mission, Fuller Theological Seminary, Pasadena in April 2002 and was subsequently published in *IBMR*, Vol. 34, No. 1, January 2010, pp. 42-5.

Appendix

Cliff College and Missiology

Cliff College has a long and rich heritage of providing Bible training to people from diverse backgrounds, for mission and evangelism. It started in 1883 in the home of its founder Thomas Champness in Bolton. He later moved into Castleton Hall at Rochdale where the work continued until he retired. The Wesleyan Methodist Church took over the work and moved the college to its current location, Calver (Derbyshire), in 1904 where more space was available. Since the beginning the College has sought to provide Biblical, Evangelical training that is both relevant and forward-thinking, with an emphasis on Scriptural Holiness.

Cliff College currently serves most Christian denominations with its training. Historically, Cliff was a Methodist Lay Training college and today it is one of two colleges of the Discipleship and Ministries Learning Network of the British Methodist Church with a student body and Faculty that is both lay and ordained and from a diverse denominational background. Its academic programmes are validated by the University of Manchester.

The College's defining characteristic has always been training in mission and evangelism. In recent years evangelism in contemporary culture, pioneer ministry and fresh expressions, and ministry among children and young people have been prioritised. The College's International Training Centre works in Nigeria, Sierra Leone and elsewhere to provide training and enable missional reflection in a number of different contexts.

The largest academic programme is the MA in Mission and missiology can be further studied at PhD level, and on the PhD in Missiology (professional doctorate) programme.

www.cliffcollege.ac.uk